1 MONTH OF
FREE
READING

at

www.ForgottenBooks.com

By purchasing this book you are
eligible for one month membership to
ForgottenBooks.com, giving you
unlimited access to our entire
collection of over 1,000,000 titles via
our web site and mobile apps.

To claim your free month visit:
www.forgottenbooks.com/free1242457

ISBN 978-0-428-53706-7
PIBN 11242457

A REPORT OF ARCHAEOLOGY AT THE ROBERT TOOMBS HOUSE HISTORIC SITE WASHINGTON, GEORGIA — 1976

by
John R. Morgan

State of Georgia
Department of Natural Resources
Parks, Recreation and Historic Sites Division
Historic Preservation Section
1981

This document has been funded with the assistance of a matching grant-in-aid from the United States Department of the Interior, Heritage Conservation and Recreation Service, through the Historic Preservation Section, Georgia Department of Natural Resources, under provisions of the National Historic Preservation Act of 1966.

A REPORT OF ARCHAEOLOGY AT THE ROBERT TOOMBS HOUSE HISTORIC SITE

WASHINGTON, GEORGIA - 1976

by

John R. Morgan

Figure 1. The Robert Toombs House, 1976
(Photograph by David J. Kaminsky)

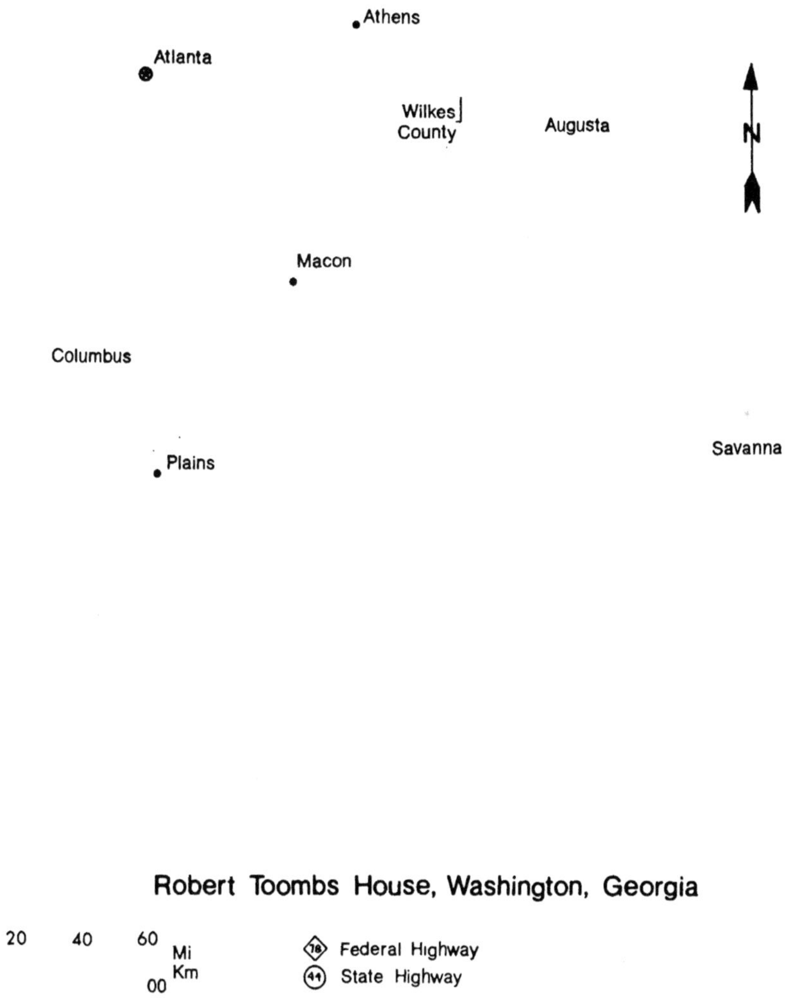

.Athens

Atlanta
●

Wilkes⌋
County   Augusta

N

Macon
●

Columbus

Savanna

. Plains
●

Robert Toombs House, Washington, Georgia

20   40   60
                Mi   ⬥⑱ Federal Highway
          00 Km   ⑪ State Highway

Figure 2. A Map of the Location of the Robert Toombs House.

Dedicated to Alston C. Waylor and the members of the archaeological crew of this project: Jim Dickey, Kenny Johnson, Harvey McKenzie, and Jack Pullen.

ACKNOWLEDGEMENTS

Any effort of research is obviously a product of more than the labor of the person whose name appears on a report. The following are some of those unnamed producers. The archaeology literally could not have been done without the work of field assistant Jim Dickey and crew members Kenny Johnson, Harvey McKenzie, and Jack Pullen. Without the direction of then Chief Administrator of State Historic Sites Alston Waylor, archaeology and restoration would have led uncoordinated schedules. Site Curator Randy Powers functioned as our ambassador to Washington, providing assistance in local matters. B.G. Grizzle, Willie Wingfield, and James Avery helped out when our numbers were insufficient or our ranks depleted. Ken Thomas and Ed Neal delineated the course of archaeology by the clarity which their work brought to defining additional needs of research. Among those who reviewed and commented on drafts of this report are Patty Deveau, Morton McInvale, Ken Thomas, Marion Hemperley, Jack Pullen, and Lew Larson. My colleagues, in spite of their own busy schedules, managed to respond to my calls for help. Awards of patience should be given my supervisor, Carole Griffith, and to our supervisor, Liz Lyon. They were co-conspirators in my goal-quest of publication by allocating time to research and write. My wife, Mary, did not see her dining room table for months. Finally, State Archaeologist Lewis H. Larson, Jr., whose professional advice and support were sought frequently and given freely, provided the impetus to complete this project. To all of these people, and to many others who contributed in ways too numerous to list, I express my deepest thanks for your patience, guidance, and, most of all, your help.

TABLE OF CONTENTS

LIST OF TABLES

LIST OF FIGURES

CHAPTER 1

INTRODUCTION

Subject of Investigation

East of the town limit of Washington, Georgia, Joel Abbot, a physician
from Ridgefield, Connecticut, was constructing a home in 1797. According to
his deed to twelve acres purchased from Micajah and Mary Williamson for sixty
dollars, Dr. Abbot was "abuilding" (Thomas 1974:45, 56). Reportedly, the
house was two stories over a raised basement (Writers' Program of the W.P.A.
1941:109; Thomas 1974:100). After Abbot's death in 1826, the house was home
for a number of residents and underwent another ownership before Robert Toombs,
a noted Georgia statesman, bought it from William L. Harris in 1837 (Thomas
1974:12-21). Toombs died in 1885 with the house remaining in the ownership of
his relatives until State acquisition in 1973 (Thomas 1974:62-4). The Georgia
Department of Natural Resources acquired the home of Robert Toombs as a component of its program to preserve and interpret the history of the state (see
Figures 1 and 2).

With State acquisition of the house came two major tasks: preserving and
interpreting the site. Historical research was initiated to document the house
and its residents, providing an inventory of information for undertaking interpretation. Architectural research was begun for two reasons. One was to as-
sess the preservation needs of the house, recommending appropriate measures for
stabilizing and restoring the nearly 200-year-old structure. The other was to
analyze the architectural history of the house. The goal of these tasks was to

provide direction for preservation and interpretation.

Origin of Problems

Results of historical research were some dubious answers to questions addressed. The majority of available sources were secondary at best. Many did
not have footnotes, citations, or bibliographies. Architectural research
brought recommendations for stabilizing foundations and controlling the climate
of the basement, among others. Architectural analysis revealed many anomalies
in the house. Windows covered over, door placements altered, mortises empty of
tenons, ceilings raised, lathing cut by different methods were just a few.
The frame of the house was obviously not a consequence of a single phase of
construction. A complex, but incomplete, picture was produced.

Given interpretive and restorative needs of the house, conflict was recognized. Solutions to interpretive problems generated by historical and architectural research could potentially be recovered from resources in the basement. The conflict was that these resources were threatened by restorative
measures necessary for preserving the house. Resources in the basement were
archaeological in nature as they were situated beneath the surface of the
ground. Measures of stabilizing foundations and controlling climate would use
techniques which would disturb, or destroy, the very resources, archaeological
ones, which might contain solutions to some of the interpretive problems. A
program for archaeologically mitigating the impact of proposed measures of
restoration was, therefore, warranted.

The problem of interpreting the Toombs House was compounded by problems of
preserving it. Historical and architectural research generated problems for
which tendered solutions were inconclusive. The house is composed of a number
of architecturally distinguishable phases. Historical research, however,

failed to substantively document this phasing or its chronological sequence. Architectural research offered a sequence for the phases based on stylistic and structural analysis. These research efforts, of course, were limited. All potential repositories of historical information were not examined, nor was the entire house dismantled for architectural scrutiny. The date of construction of what was stylistically analyzed as the oldest phase of the house, 1797, was based on a single primary source (Deeds, Wilkes County, Georgia, Book QQ, p. 243), only suggestive in content. Removal of appendages from the house was based on oral tradition, secondary documentary sources, and indicative architectural features. Finally, oral tradition mentioned in a secondary source asserts that the Abbot portion of the house was moved back from the road, supposedly East Robert Toombs Avenue. Tentative historical and architectural conclusions were drawn.

Compounding the problems highlighted by historical and architectural research were the results of architectural analysis of the physical integrity of the house. Foundations needed to be stabilized by waterproofing and repairing them. Installation of a system to control the climate of the basement required ducts placed beneath the floor of the basement. For reasons involving public access (safety, interpretation, and convenience), some areas of the basement were to be altered by adaptive use. These restorative measures threatened resources thought to have potential for solving some of the interpretive problems. At the Toombs House, interpretation and preservation conflicted. To preserve the house, resources potentially containing solutions to problems of interpretation were threatened with disturbance and destruction by preservation measures.

No previous archaeology at the Toombs House was reported; therefore, the archaeological potential of the basement was assumed. Imminent loss of potential resources of information for solving historical and architectural problems had to be dealt with. Preservation as a strategy to stabilize the house could not be permitted to result in the loss of a portion of the values for which the house was acquired. Resources were assumed to exist beneath the ground in the basement. Archaeology was the appropriate means of retrieving pertinent information from these kinds of resources.

Statement of Purpose

The purpose of archaeology at the Toombs House was to mitigate the destructive effects of proposed restorative measures on assumed archaeological resources in the basement. Four problems identified by preceding research (historical and architectural) oriented archaeological strategy: number of phases of construction, sequence and dates of identified phases, removal of appendages, and relocation of a portion of the house. In addition to this mitigative focus, a problem concerning season of construction provided another focus. Resources to be investigated for mitigative purposes also offered information about seasonality of construction of foundations. A final aspect of purpose was to appropriately treat unexpected resources which might be encountered while investigating the assumed resources. The five identified problems for purposes of investigation will be formulated as working hypotheses.

These working hypotheses (Kaplan 1964:88-9) provide direction for data collection. The first four are based on the preceding research conducted for the Toombs House (Neal 1976; Thomas 1974). The fifth is based on preparatory research conducted as a part of planning archaeology for this house. The discovery of unexpected resources is treated merely by anticipation. The working hypotheses are outlined as follows.

Working Hypotheses

Hypothesis 1:   The Toombs House was constructed in four temporally distinct
                phases.

Test Implications

1.   The configurations of footing trenches and associated features will
     delineate phases of construction.

2.   Foundations of each phase of construction are composed of distinctive
     building materials.

3.   Building practices of each phase of construction are distinguishable
     from other phases.

4.   Foundations of distinct phases of construction will not be structur-
     ally interlocked.

5.   Dates derived from analysis of ceramics recovered from features result-
     ing from construction, such as footing trenches, will temporally dis-
     tinguish building phases.

Hypothesis 2:   The sequence of phases of construction is first, Room A-4/5/6/7;
                second, Room A-9/10; third, Room A-1/2, and fourth, Room A-8
                (see Figures 3 and 17).

Test Implications

1.   The configurations of footing trenches and associated features of con-
     struction will delineate a sequence.

2.   Foundations of each phase of construction are composed of temporally
     distinctive materials.

3.   Building practices of each phase of construction are temporally dis-
     tinguishable from other phases.

4. Dates derived from analysis of ceramics recovered from construction features, such as footing trenches, will temporally order the phases.

Hypothesis 3: Prior to the construction of Room A-1/2, an appendage was attached to the east side of Room A-4/5/6.

Test Implications

1. Remnants of structural features will be encountered such as footings, piers, foundations, posts, steps, walkways, drip lines, etc.
2. Remnants of construction features will be encountered such as footing trenches, post holes, trash pits, treadways, etc.
3. Temporally diagnostic artifacts associated with construction and structural remnants of an appendage east of Room A-4/5/6 will be recovered.

Hypothesis 4: A portion of the house, Room A-4/5/6/7 (the Abbot house) was moved back, i.e., south, from East Robert Toombs Avenue.

Test Implications

1. Remnants of features resulting from the activity of moving the house, such as unusually placed trenches, post holes, pits, treadways, foundations, etc., will be found.
2. Anomalous footing trenches, footings, foundations, or associated features resulting from relocation of the house will be detected.
3. Evidence of previous use of the site of the Toombs House.
4. Circumstantial historic evidence for relocation of the Abbot portion of the house.
5. Dates derived from analysis of artifacts recovered from features identified as consequences of house-moving activities will cluster around 1797.

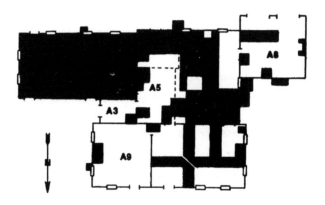

Room Designation Scheme And Area Excavated

Scale:

0 5 10   20   30 Ft
                      M
0   5   10

Legend:

■ Area Excavated
⊢ ⊢ Doorway
▭ Window
⊓ Fireplace or Base
- - - - Partitions Removed
        in Room A4,5,6

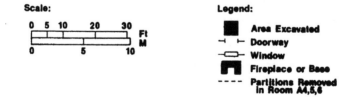

TOOMBS HOUSE 1976

Figure 3. A Plan of the Basement of the Toombs House.

These hypotheses treat interpretive problems of the Toombs House generated by preceding research. A fifth working hypothesis is not a consequence of responding to interpretive-restorative needs. It is research-oriented in a broader sense because results are not site-specific.

Hypothesis 5: The form and placement of a footing trench relative to the footing contained may indicate the season in which a foundation was constructed.

Test Implications

1. Footing trenches will be present for the foundations of the Toombs House.

2. Footing trenches with the form of expanded width relative to the interior or exterior face of contained footings will be found.

Data requirements for these hypotheses will not be discussed in detail here. The sources of data are primarily archaeological. Historical sources play a role in the fourth hypothesis because some circumstances had not been collectively treated in preceding research. Data requirements will be discussed in the section on "Methods, Techniques, and Data Requirements."

Scope of Investigation

The scope of archaeology at the Toombs House had a number of delimitations. Archaeology was included as a part of the restoration funded with grant assistance from Heritage Conservation and Recreation Service, U.S. Department of the Interior. Scope, therefore, was restricted to the basement. Restoration had a deadline for expending funds and completing work. Archaeology focused on those problems for which solutions were assumed to pertain to resources threatened by restorative measures. Due to the dearth of reported archaeology on Georgia

piedmont historic sites, comparative analysis is absent. This situation will
be elaborated in the section on "Review of Related Literature."

Theoretical Framework

This discussion of theoretical framework will be brief. The objective is
to present some of the author's perspective so that readers may have some idea
of his theoretical orientation. No elaboration of theory, nor its role in historical archaeology, follows. This is left to Stanley South and others who
have so appropriately generated discussion and debate of the relationship of
theory to historical archaeology (Cleland and Fitting 1968; Dollar 1968, 1971;
Harrington 1955; Noel Hume 1969; South 1968, 1977; Walker 1967' 1968, 1970).

South says that historical archaeology must do more than descriptively report findings of investigation. Archaeological results have to be more than
catalogues of retrieved artifacts. Contributing to the advancement of archaeology requires more knowledge to be returned to the "bank" of archaeological information than is withdrawn from it (South 1974a:5, 1977:308-13). In an expli-
cit, well-thought-out manner, problems warranting archaeological investigation
must be posed in such a way that "particularistic" solutions are not the sole
product. (For a discussion of "particularistic archaeology," see South 1977:
8-12). Problems must be formulated in such a manner that solutions elucidate
processes of cultural behavior. Archaeologists want to understand past cultural behavior which they cannot observe directly. They must infer through
properly formulated problems processes of past behavior based on identifying,
recording, and analyzing spatial and contextual relationships of remaining behavioral products comprising the archaeological record. Patterns of relationships among these behavioral products must be detected, demonstrated, and interpreted. A fundamental problem confronting archaeologists is how to

correctly and sufficiently infer the behavioral processes which produced the archaeologically derived patterns of material remains (Smith 1978:xvii). An inferred process, of course, must be substantiated by evidence retrieved archaeologically, in addition to support garnered by preparatory and comparative research. Moreover, solutions, problems, and means for inferring those behavioral processes must be verified. In quest of a solution, new knowledge is sought. It may concern problems, solutions, means, or all three. If this knowledge is acquired, then new problems arise. However, previous problems, solutions, and means cannot be assumed correct or sufficient. With the goal of advancing archaeological knowledge, verification of previous problems, solutions, and means must be undertaken.

As archaeologists cannot create archaeological sites under laboratory conditions for testing, they have to repeatedly apply problems, solutions, or means to new sites and new conditions. This way problems, solutions, and means may be refined or refuted. Mario Bunge, a philosopher of science, asserts that the goal of science is the ceaseless perfecting of its chief products (theories) and means (techniques) (1967:30).

Archaeology at the Toombs House was formulated and conducted on a basis of an anthropological orientation. Its objective was more than that of supplementing historical and architectural research. The presence or absence of evidence of particular consequences of past behavior is informative. Was a room removed from this side of the house? Was this room built before that one? When was this portion of the house built? Was this portion of the house relocated? Beyond specific questions about the house are anthropological problems of cultural processes. At this house, can knowledge of processes of cultural behavior be derived from the archaeological resources? If patterns are detected among the remains of past behavior, then why do such patterns exist here? Are these patterns corroborative of an identified cultural process or indicative of a previously unknown process? Are the means of identifying cultural processes the correct ones? Are they sufficient? The fundamental problem for archaeology is how to identify adequately and correctly the processes of cultural behavior which resulted in products of archaeological interest. The basic problem for any form of inquiry is how to insure that the problem investigated, the methods used, and the solutions derived are correct and sufficient. At the Toombs House, the opportunity to research major processual problems at the site was not possible due to limitations imposed by the funding source. However, a minor problem of research was generated which could be attacked using the methods and techniques for meeting historical and architectural needs. In addition, the chance to test a recently developed analytical technique under a new condition was available. An attempt to aid in perfecting the technique was undertaken: another instance of application.

Some Basic Assumptions

Archaeology is a formal method of investigation with a set of techniques developed to recover information from a particular kind of resource.

The resources of information to which archaeology is applicable are those products of cultural behavior surviving in the ground.

Segments of past cultural behavior are preserved in products and the contexts of those products.

This investigation of surviving products of cultural behavior by means of archaeology uses concepts and theory developed in anthropology.

The anthropological approach used is an evolutionary one based on the goal of understanding cultural processes inferred from demonstrated patterns and laws derived archaeologically.

Behavioral processes active in the past are still going on today.

Some human behavior is patterned.

A cursory account of theoretical orientation has been offered; now an examination of some fundamental terms is in order.

Some Fundamental Terms

To aid in our understanding of the sources from which we expect to retrieve data pertaining to the working hypotheses, the terms "foundation," 'footing," and "footing trench" must be examined. The main archaeological resources of the Toombs House investigation are footing trenches (also called builder's trenches) and associated features of footings and foundations (South 1972:82). Data pertinent to hypotheses 1, 2, 3, and 5 may be derived from these resources which were threatened by proposed restoration measures. This research, therefore, was conducted for the purpose of gathering historical and contemporary information about footing trenches and associated features. Derived information would provide a basis on which to develop strategies and tactics for recovering data relevant to the test implications of the working hypotheses. First, an examination of definitions of footing trench, footing, and foundation was done to obtain some idea of the role of these terms in past and present usage. Second, a comparison of historical and contemporary discussions of footing trenches, footings, and foundations was undertaken to assure consistency of jargon and of application to constructional activities. We will examine historical and contemporary literature for this information.

Moxon, in his _Mechanick Exercises_ (1703:254-5), discussed the terms "foundation," "footing," and "trenches," but no formal definitions were included. Apparently, definition of these terms was assumed, reflecting their establishment in the jargon of the construction trade. However, a few years later,

Neve, in his City and Country Purchaser, defined foundation as "the lowest part of a Building (generally laid under Ground) upon which the Walls of the superstructure are rais'd" (1726:134). Neve emphasized the importance of foundations by remarking that "for if the Foundation happens to dance, t'will marr all the Mirth in the House" (1726:134). The terms "footing" and "trench" are unmentioned. Salmon, in 1734, defined a foundation as "the lowest part of a Building (generally laid under ground) upon which the Wall of the Superstructure are raised" (1734:129). The similarity to Neve's definition depicts tradition. Pain stated that "the foundations are properly called the basis of the building, the part of it under ground which sustains the whole Building above" (1762:1). "Footing" and "trench" are absent from his discussion. Lafever, however, in his The Modern Builder's Guide, defined "footings" as "projecting courses of stone, without the naked superincumbent part, and which are laid in order to rest the wall firmly on its base" (1833:121). "Foundation" and "trench" are undefined. Godwin, in an 1838 article in Architectural Magazine, discussed construction. He mentioned foundations, footings, and trenches in lectures for architectural students, but he did not define them (1838:250-5). Even at the training level, these terms are sufficiently established in the jargon of the trade, requiring no definitive discussion.

In two popular publications of the early 1800's, which focus more on architecture than construction, the terms are briefly treated. Loudon, in Encyclopedia of Cottage, Farm and Villa Architecture and Furniture (1839), did not discuss "footing," "foundation," or "trench." His "Glossorial Index" contains the listing "footings, foundations," but no page numbers are given, as are other entries; the "General Index" contains no entry for any of the terms. In a discussion of walls, Loudon stated that solidarity was dependent "on the stability and security of their foundations" (1839:1107-8), a remark which acknowledged their importance but assumed **any** definition. Downing mentioned "foundation" in that it "must be formed of stone or burnt brick;" none of the terms was defined **(1850:56)**.

This brief look at the history of the terms footing, foundation, and trench is not exhaustive, but some understanding of the terms and their role in the trade jargon is gained. The historical literature indicates their axiomatic role in the trade jargon of construction. For architecture, the role of the terms by their almost complete absence from period literature is a matter of priority with substantive consideration left to construction rather than design. An examination of some builder's guides and manuals of the 1700's and 1800's found no definitions or discussions of the terms (Downing 1850, 1967; Gibbs 1728; Halfpenny 1725, 1730; Langley 1727, 1746, 1750, 1757; Robinson 1733). The publications focused on matters of design, not fundamentals of construction. Knowledge about footings, foundations, and trenches was conveyed from teacher to apprentice at the building site, not in a text or a classroom.

For contemporary literature, only a cursory look is possible. The vast number of builder's manuals and guides in the age of "do-it'yourself" prohibits an indepth study. For our purpose, nothing more is needed, for we are seeking suggestions of trends. To begin with a standard of the building trade is appropriate.

In Audel's Masons and Builders Guide #2 (Graham 1924:1,847; 1,850), two of the terms are defined:

> Footings. This is the lowest part of the foundation and is that part which transmits the weight of the building and loads coming on it to the ground at the bottom of the excavation.

> Foundation Walls. By definition, foundation walls are those walls below the grade line of the building that support the super-structure.

Other publications examined contained definitions corresponding with these (Crispin 1942; Harris 1975; Putnam and Carlson 1974; Tweney and Hughes 1942; Vollmer 1967). A point of clarification of the relationship of footing to foundation was garnered from this examination and warrants discussion.

As can be inferred from the definitions from Graham (1924), a footing is a part of a foundation (Ulrey 1970:35). The question then arises as to why the terminological distinction. The answer lies in understanding the problem of proportioning the weight of the structure transmitted by the wall or pier of the foundation evenly over a footing (Kidder and Parker 1956:154; Putnam and Carlson 1974:202; Ulrey 1970:32). Footings, having greater horizontal dimension than foundation walls or piers, spread the borne weight to the ground beneath them. The purpose of the footing is to transmit the load to the earth in such a manner that settlement is negligible or is uniform under all portions of the structure (Dietz 1974:35; Goodman and Karol 1968:113). Foundations function to support the structure with a special portion of them, the footings, serving to distribute weight evenly over a larger area. Foundations, therefore, consist of two parts: piers/walls and footings (Moxon 1703:225; Dietz 1974:35).

Little information about trenches for footings (builder's trenches) was found, but inferring from building prescriptions gives some indications. Moxon mentioned "trenches" being dug to ascertain the weight-bearing adequacy of soils ((1703:254). He also stated that "all Walls ought to have a Basis, or Footing, at least 4 inches on a side broader than the thickness of the wall" (Moxon 1703:255). Neve, in discussing a building site, said that it "be of solid Earth, you may dig for the Foundations, so far as a discreet Architect shall think requisite for the Quality of the Building, and the Soundness of the Earth" (1726:135). Salmon (1734), as we said, passingly mentioned only foundations. Pain prescribed that foundations -- that is, footings -- ought to be twice as thick (wide) as the wall to be built on them (1762:1), suggesting width of a trench but no hint of depth. Godwin specified that adequate footings be nine inches wider on each side than the foundation wall and twelve inches in thickness (1838:255).

Not until contemporary literature is examined are more details gained about trenches for footings. The following discussion, however, is tempered by pragmatics of the building trade. Among builders, a rule-of-thumb is used for determining width and thickness of footings if no building codes exist (Dietz 1974:35; Maldon 1977:98; Ulrey 1970:34). A footing will be constructed as follows: width equals two times the thickness of the wall; thickness of footing equals the thickness of the wall (U.S. Navy 1972:295; see Figure 4). With some idea of the dimensions of footings, we can speculate about footing trenches.

Given that any footing trench minimally has to be as wide as the footing, some contemporary sources were examined for additional clues. Kidder and Parker state that a footing should be at least eight inches wider than the wall supported; for a structure of two stories or more, a footing should be twelve inches wide (1956:234). Maldon gives a guide that a footing should be twice as wide as the wall it bears (1977:98). Dietz says a footing should be three or four inches greater on each side than the wall above (1974:35). Badzinski states that the thickness of a footing should be twice the width of a wall but should not project more than six inches beyond the wall unless it is reinforced (1972:5-6). In other words, the width of a footing trench is sufficient to accommodate the footing, which is dimensionally proportional to the thickness of the wall or pier to be borne by that footing. Only a single source was located which gave any hint of a trench being wider than necessary to receive a footing. A U.S. Navy construction manual states that for cellars or basements, the excavations shall extend two feet outside of all basement wall planes (1972:53).

Attempting to develop expectations for the depth of a footing trench is difficult as a number of variables are involved. Prescriptions are often so general as to be uninformative. For example, excavation will be carried down to a surface which will permit equal settlement of the structure (Graham 1924: 1, 847). Apparently, equal distribution of weight on the soil is critical, but a number of other variables have to be considered. In some areas, climate is a factor: footings should be some inches below the frost line (Maldon 1977: 98; Sowers and Sowers 1961:151). Soils are critical, because the type of foundation used is closely related to its supporting properties (McCarthy 1977: 337). The bearing capacity of soils depends on their composition, compactness, and moisture content (Hool 1913:217). Neve directed that the building site "be firm solid Earth," but the depth of excavation was reduced to a rule: "a sixth part of the height of the Fabrick" (1726:135). Moxon stated that the builder must be sure that the soils are "fit to bear the weight which is to be set upon them" (1703:254). Regarding the relationship between the weight of the structure and the bearing capacity of soils, ordinary soils will usually bear more weight the greater their depth below the surface because they are more condensed (Hool 1913:217). Kidder and Parker state that footings should be at least eight inches thick; and for buildings of more than two stories, a thickness of at least twelve inches (1956:235, Table I). Another factor is one called "live load," that is, the weight of traffic to be borne by a struc-ture (McCarthy 1977:337; Buchanan 1976). Treatment of this factor in many sources was of a general nature (Dietz 1974 35; Maldon 1977:98; U.S. Navy 1972: 295; Godwin 1838:255; Graham 1924:1,847). For most residential structures,

footings are seldom designed but built by rule-of-thumb (Dietz 1974:35). The
depth of a footing trench then seems to be dependent on two variables: (1)
characteristics of the structure, and (2) composition of the soil (Sowers and
Sowers 1961:150).

As can be seen, the dimensions of footing trenches, width and depth, are
a consequence of rule-of-thumb construction for residences. From a broad historical perspective, Buchanan generalizes for early American construction that
for buildings without cellars foundations were seldom deeper than eighteen
inches below the surface of the ground (1976:58-9). The thickness of foundations varied from nine to twenty-six inches, proportional of the size and function of the structure resting on them (Buchanan 1976:58-9).

Based on this research, some expectations of dimensions of footings and
footing trenches can be formed. Regarding the width of footings, a foundation
wall or pier has to bear uniformly on everything which supports it, the footing
as well as the soil. The foundation, then, is centered laterally on a footing
to evenly distribute the load to be borne (Dietz 1974:35; McCarthy 1977:339).
We may, therefore, expect that a footing will extend equal distances beyond
the vertical planes of the foundation wall which it supports. The sum of
these extensions, and only them, will equal the width of wall supported by the
footing (Maldon 1977:98; Moxon 1703:255; Pain 1762:1; U.S. Navy 1972:295). Or
stated another way, the width of a footing will be twice the width of the wall
supported (see Figure 4).

Forming expectations for thickness, that is, the vertical dimension, of a
footing is more difficult. The climatic necessity of building beneath a frost
line is not a factor in Washington, Georgia. Soil at the Toombs House should
not have been a problem as the subsoil is a widely occurring, dense clay (Long
1916:21). From our preparatory research, we have learned that generally a

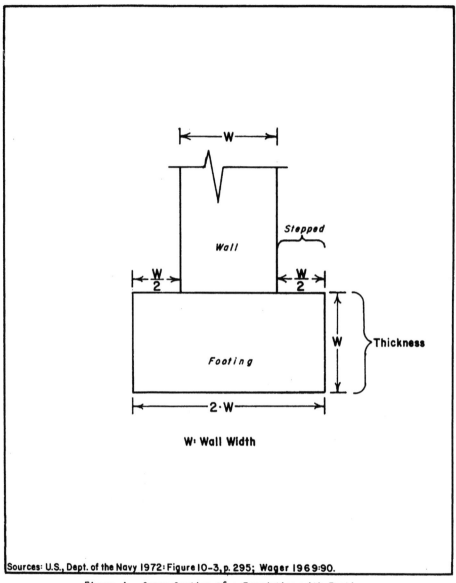

Figure 4. Cross-Section of a Foundation with Footing
Illustrating Rule-of-the-Thumb Dimensions.

footing will be as thick as the supported wall is wide (see Figure 4; Dietz 1974:35; Maldon 1977:98; Wagner 1969:90). Nevertheless, for the Toombs House, some variables must be considered: the weight of the structure, the forms of support, and the composition of footing materials. The house is a full two-story frame, except for Rooms A-1/2 and A-8, over a raised basement supported by brick walls and piers resting on brick footings.

Dietz states that, for most residences, foundations are built according to a rule-of-thumb (1974:35; for example, see Figure 4), but others have suggested exceptions to this rule (Kidder and Parker 1956:234, McCarthy 1977:337; Neve 1726:135; Ulrey 1970:32). Given that the walls and piers of the Toombs House foundation are measureable, their dimensions may not be a basis on which to form reliable expectations as to the thickness of footings or the depth of footing trenches. In addition to walls, a portion of the house, Room A-4/5/6 and part of A-8 (see Figures 3 and 17), is built on piers. The use of piers may be a consequence of factors of construction, environment, style, or some combination. For construction, two variables may be involved, soils and costs. One, setting a structure on piers could indicate that soil conditions vary; therefore, the weight is concentrated on areas judged as adequate, spanning those of questionable nature (Harris 1975:360; Moxon 1703:256). Two, constructing piers uses less labor and materials, thus reducing costs (Moxon 1703: 256; U.S. Navy 1972:295). Pertinent environmental factors may be a consequence of latitude. A temperate climate accompanied by high humidity might result in the builder elevating a house to catch favorable breezes, while removing wooden framing from the damaging effects of proximity to damp soil, or flooding (Linley 1972:59; Morrison 1952:259; Nichols 1957:39, 125, 127). Stylistic factors may be those of status. In discussing the Greek Revival house in Georgia, Zelinsky comments that all are set on high basements, "thus sharply

set off from the cellarless homes of the middle and lower classes" (1954:9).
Linley speaks of the "unexcelled view of the countryside" afforded residents
of a home in Hancock County with a raised main floor (1972:59).

Regardless of the needs of construction or the desires of the builder-
owner, footings of piers receive a concentration of structural weight (Harris
1975:360). Two responses to this focus of thought may be anticipated. Dimensions of footings may be increased, or material with a higher density may be
used. Footings constructed of the same material as the pier it supports will
probably have greater dimensions than footings supporting a wall. Along its
length, a wall continuously distributes its weight through the footing. The
larger footing of a pier provides more surface over which to distribute the
weight concentrated by the pier. On the other hand, a material of higher density than that of the pier may be used in the footing (Neve 1726:136). In such
a case, the variance from the rule-of-thumb may not be as great, in spite of
concentrated weight. The higher density material probably would not require
as much additional surface to distribute the concentration of weight.

As the house is supported by both forms of foundation, pier and wall, the
dimensions of footings of the respective forms may differ. The rule-of-thumb
does not distinguish between forms of foundations; thus, the width of a pier
may not be a reliable indicator of the dimensions of its footing or a footing
trench. With the composition of footings unknown, expectations for dimensions
are uncertain.

Plan of the Report

The plan of the report consists of six major sections, beginning with a
review of literature. Unfortunately, little historic archaeology has been
conducted in the Georgia piedmont. Of that which has, none was informative to

this investigation. In place of this void, other sources were examined in an attempt to learn more about the Toombs House: state, county, and local histories of the Washington-Wilkes area; three biographies of Toombs, and some reports of architectural surveys. The most informative sources, nevertheless, were products of preceding research at the Toombs House. After this review of literature, the preparatory research conducted for developing natural and cultural parameters of environment is discussed. The subsection on cultural setting is elaborated in an attempt to understand the Washington to which Joel Abbot migrated. This section is followed by one detailing methods, techniques, and data requirements of archaeology at the Toombs House. Next, a section on analysis treats the results of archaeological excavation. The analysis section is followed by one discussing general results. Conclusions of a general nature comprise the last section.

CHAPTER 2

REVIEW OF LITERATURE

Factors Limiting Review

For the Toombs House archaeology, the task of reviewing pertinent literature is delimited by three factors. The first is the focus of the investigation as defined by its mitigatory purpose. The thrust of this effort is to
meet needs of preservation and interpretation, not of research. The second is
the nature of the resource, an extant, Euro-American urban residence of the
late-eighteenth to early-nineteenth century on the Georgia piedmont. The
third factor is the dearth of reported research for comparative study. The
amount of reported historic archaeology on the piedmont of Georgia is small.
Even less frequent are reports of archaeology conducted at extant Euro-American urban residences of the Toombs House period. Absent are reports of archaeology conducted at sites comparable to the Toombs House. A table was prepared
which summarizes this situation (see Table 1). In the absence of comparative
literature, a review of other sources for information about the Toombs House
was undertaken.

Historical Literature

Historical literature above a county-wide scope was uninformative about
the Toombs House. Histories of Georgia cursorily associate Toombs with his
Washington home, especially in accounts of Union troops attempting to capture
him there in 1865 (Cooper 1938; Coulter 1960; Howell 1926; Johnson 1938;
Knight 1917). Other state histories do not mention the house (Avery 1881;

- 23 -

TABLE 1

A SUMMARY OF REPORTS OF HISTORICAL ARCHAEOLOGY CONDUCTED ON THE GEORGIA PIEDMONT

Author and date	Site name	County	Type of resource	Condition of resource	Period	Setting	Purpose of archaeology	Place of archaeology	Level of work
Carrillo 1972	Fort Hawkins	Bibb	Fort	Subsurface remains	1806	Urban: Macon	Identify fortifications	Palisade line	Subsurface testing
DeBaillou 1954	White House	Richmond	House	Restored house	1747	Urban: Augusta	Identification/ Interpretation	Yard	Subsurface testing
Garrow 1979	Rock House	McDuffie	House	Abandoned & delapidated	c. 1785	Rural	Restoration/ Interpretation	Basement & appendages	Survey & testing
Garrow 1980	E. Winn House	Gwinnett	House	Deteriorating residence	c. 1812	Rural	Restoration/ Interpretation	Crawl space & grounds	Survey & testing
Gresham, et al. 1981	Newton Factory	Newton	Mills	Ruins	1830-1920	Rural	Inventory & Evaluation	Project boundary	Survey & testing
Kelly 1939	Macon Trading Post	Bibb	Fort/trading post	Subsurface remains	1680-1718	Rural	Identification/ Interpretation	Limits of feature	Excavation
Kelso 1971	Traveler's Rest	Stephens	Inn & Residence	Restored structure	c. 1815	Rural	Restoration/ Interpretation	Cellar & grounds	Testing & excavation
Mistovich & Blair 1979	Overlook Mansion	Bibb	House	Residence	1836	Urban: Macon	Restoration/ Interpretation	House & grounds	Testing & excavation
Wood, K. 1980b	Gilmer House	Oglethorpe	House	Foundation/ cellar ruins	c. 1800	Rural	Mitigation	Foundations & grounds	Testing & excavation
Wood, K. 1980a	C. W. Long House	Madison	House	Abandoned & delapidated	c. 1820	Urban: Danielsville	Restoration/ Interpretation	Grounds	Survey & testing

TABLE 1-(continued)

Author and date	Site name	County	Type of resource	Condition of resource	Period	Setting	Purpose of archaeology	Place of archaeology	Level of work
Wood, W.D. 1979	Twin Oaks	Meriwether	House	Residence	c. 1857	Rural	Interpretation & planning	steps of house & grounds	Survey & testing
Wood, W.D. 1980	Bledsoe-Green house	Putnam	House site	Subsurface remains	c. 1814	Urban: Eatonton	Identification & planning	grounds	Survey & testing

Coleman 1960, 1977). Three biographies of Toombs have been published, but no pertinent information about the house is contained in any of them (Phillips 1913; Stovall 1892; Thompson 1966).

At the county-wide scope, there are a number of publications about Wilkes County (see Purdie 1979:75-7). Of these, two are informative about the Toombs House. In her history, Bowen (1950:102) related five significant items of information about the house. One, a portion of the Toombs House, that which was built by Abbot, was "moved back" from the street. Two, William L. Harris, an owner of the house, "built the front rooms." Three, Toombs added to the house "the colonade, and then the western living wing and finally the eastern wing, and kitchen." Four, DuBose "remodelled the interior" and "built the green-house." Five, a part of the Abbot portion of the house "was moved to what is now the property of Mr. Lowe on Alexander Avenue" (see Writers' Program of the W.P.A. 1941:104, #17). Bowen's sources were oral tradition apparently gathered from local informants. The other publication relates that "the main body, a two-story structure on a high basement, was built in 1794 by Dr. Joel Abbot," but no source of this information is cited (Writers' Program of the W.P.A. 1941:109). Also included are the structural alterations mentioned by Bowen (1950), but they, too, are uncited.

Of a scope more specific than county history, only one report treats solely the Toombs House. For the Department of Natural Resources, historical research was conducted for interpretive purposes. Thomas' report, The Robert Toombs House (1974), is a product of this effort. A look at other sources of information besides history is warranted as we are dealing with an extant building.

Architectural Literature

Architectural research at the statewide scope provides a number of
sources of pertinent information about the Toombs House. In a report of the
Historic American Buildings Survey (1941), the Toombs House was inventoried in
1934. Two photographs were taken and a brief description written (1941:95).
Nichols (1957:197), in his Early Architecture of Georgia, illustrates the
Toombs House with a captioned photograph: "Robert Toombs House, Washington,
about 1794, porticos added after 1837." Later, in his Architecture of Georgia,
Nichols has a photograph of the house with a revised caption: "Dr. Joel Abbott
House . . . 1797; enlarged to present appearance by Robert Toombs, 1840-60"
(1976:287). The Toombs House, in 1972, was listed in the National Register of
Historic Places as part of a statewide program of structural inventory (Georgia Department of Natural Resources 1972). The National Register form contains a summary of historical and architectural information, citing sources
previously discussed. Highlights of this summary are of interest in this review: the oldest portion, part of a two-story plantation plain house, was
built in 1797 by Dr. Joel Abbott; the front part of the house was obviously
added to an older structure; projecting wings were added to the oldest portion
before and after the Civil War; and a monumental Doric portico was added during Toombs' ownership.

At a sub-state scope, two architectural surveys of portions of the
Georgia piedmont have been published, but neither includes Wilkes County. One,
however, treats houses of Oglethorpe County, which borders Wilkes on the north-
west (Rogers 1971). The other, a survey of Baldwin, Hancock, Jasper, Johnson,
Putnam, Washington, and Wilkinson counties, focuses on an area southwest of
Wilkes County (Linley 1972). Next, the architecture of Wilkes County is

addressed at the countywide scope.

On this scope, two sources mention the Toombs House with regard to architecture. Previously discussed, The Story of Washington-Wilkes (Writers' Program of the W.P.A. 1941) contains a chapter treating the architecture as well as the history of a number of structures in Washington, among them the Toombs House (Writers' Program 1941:109-10). The report of a countywide structural survey conducted under the auspices of the State Historic Preservation Office inventoried the Toombs House (Reap 1977). It is structure number sixty in the report. No additional information beyond that already mentioned is reported, but the date of the house is given as c. 1837. Neither source provides any new information.

As far as architectural research is concerned, the most informative study of the house was conducted by architect Ed Neal. In 1975, the Department of Natural Resources contracted for his services to provide plans and specifications for a historic restoration of the house. Neal examined the house, attempting to determine the sequence of construction, the periods of major alterations, and the appearances of the house as it changed. This study was formalized in line drawings of the house, past, present, and proposed. Neal's efforts provided more reliable information about the house than any other record examined during this review.

Informative Sources

Few of these sources provided sufficient information on which to formulate strategy or select tactics for this archaeology. The exceptions of Thomas (1974) and Neal (1976) came with State acquisition of the house. Thomas' research of owners and residents as well as the history of the house and land produced a historical context. Neal's structural analysis and recommendations for restoration refined some of the interpretive problems Thomas identified. Considered together, these efforts highlighted problems to be addressed by additional investigation. A brief account of their contributions follows.

Thomas documented through a variety of historical sources this sequence of events. In 1797, Joel Abbot constructed a two-story house on a high basement. During the ownership of William L. Harris, 1834-1837, the Abbot house was moved back from the road, presumably East Robert Toombs Avenue. Harris added a wing on the north side of the Abbot portion, reorienting the front of the house from west to north. In 1837, Robert Toombs purchased the house, modifying it at unknown dates by adding Doric columns and removing an appendage from the Abbot portion for relocation off the property. The site of relocation was reportedly the David Tobouren house in Washington (205 South Alexander Avenue). This outline served as a basis for Neal's analytic efforts.

Neal observed numerous architectural attributes indicative of structural changes throughout the house. Variations in thickness of foundation piers and walls in the basement suggested phases of construction. The size and composition of bricks of this masonry also varied. Evidence of a former stair line on lathing of a hall was discovered when plaster was removed. Mortises on header beams empty of studs and joists indicated possible removal of a wall, possibly an appendage. Alteration of window and door placements, weatherboard on an interior wall, secondhand material used in framing, ceiling raised in a room, charred framing members, all demonstrated the house had not been static. These attributes of change were obvious once exposed, but their origin, meaning, and sequence were not. Some of the implications of historical research for changes in the house were substantiated by architectural analysis. Understanding many of these attributes, however, was inconclusive due to their interpretive ambiguity. As the house could not be entirely disassembled for analysis because of the obvious reasons of money and time, much of the architecturally derived information was corroborative of change but inconclusive of origin, meaning, or sequence.

Similar Problems at Comparable Sites

Unfortunately for archaeology at the Toombs House, similar problems at comparable structures have not been addressed. Obviously, the situation at the Toombs House is not unique. However, archaeology as a means of retrieving information at houses with similar problems has been ignored, or the potential unrecognized. Here, at a public historic site, this was not the case. All of the values of the Toombs House, architectural, historical, and archaeological, had to be considered in planning restoration and interpretation. Thus, for dealing with inconclusive solutions of problems identified by historical and architectural research, archaeological resources, as yet untapped, had to be investigated. This was particularly the case in the light of their imminent loss due to measures recommended for preserving some of the values for which the house was acquired.

Figure 5. Yonge Map of the Northern Portion of the "New Purchase" of 1773 (Surveyor General Department, Office of the Secretary of State).

PREPARATORY RESEARCH

Natural Environment

Any discussion of the natural environment of the Washington-Wilkes area in the historic period must begin with William Bartram's observations of the "New Purchase," the Indian cession of 1773 (see Figure 5). He was accompanying the surveyors demarcating the boundary of this acquisition.

> This new ceded country promises plenty & felicity. The lands on the River are generally rich & those of its almost innumerable branches agreeable and healthy situations, especially for small farms, every where little mounts & hills to build on & beneath them rich level land fit for corn & any grain with delightful glittering streams of running water through cain bottoms, oroper for meadows, with abundance of water brooks for mills. The hills suit extremely well for vineyards & olives as nature points out by the abundant produce of fruitful grape vine, native mulberry trees of an excellent quality for silk. Any of this land would produce indigo & no country is more proper for the culture of almost all kinds of fruits (Bartram 1943:144).

Later, in 1849, White described a Wilkes County of about the size we know it today:

> The surface of the country is undulating. The soil is various. The lands of the best kind are on Little and Broad rivers, and on the creeks generally, having a red soil, adapted to cotton and the different grains. The light sandy lands produce well for a few years (1849:608).

With these descriptions in mind, we shall examine this country of "plenty & felicity" more closely.

Physiography

Physiographically, Wilkes County is located in the Washington Slope District, Southern Piedmont Section of the Piedmont Province (Clark and Zisa 1976; LaForge 1925; Thornbury 1965; see Figure 6). The district is bounded on the south by the fall line and on the east by the Savannah River. Its western boundary corresponds to the drainage divide between the Gulf of Mexico and the Atlantic Ocean. On the north, it is bounded by the Winder Slope District. A gently undulating surface, which descends from an elevation of 210 meters on the northern margin to about 170 meters on the south, characterizes the district. Streams occupy broad, shallow valleys with long, gentle side slopes separated by broad, rounded divides. Throughout the district, relief is fifteen to thirty meters, except near the Ocmulgee River on the western boundary.

More specifically, Wilkes County has a rolling topography with numerous creeks which have cut valleys fifteen to thirty meters below crests of intervening ridges. Most of the county is about 170 meters above sea level. Broad and Little rivers, northern and southern boundaries of the county, drain southeasterly to the Savannah River. Between these rivers, a gently undulating divide extends east-west through the county. Washington is centrally located in the county on the crest of this divide.

Geology

The geology of the piedmont consists of deeply weathered bedrock which is composed of ancient sediments. These sediments are intruded by granites and related basic and ultrabasic rock. Once shales and sandstones, they are now quartzites, schists, and slate (Atwood 1940; Fenneman 1938; Hunt 1967). This discussion applies to Wilkes County in general.

Soil

Soils of the piedmont are red with sandy clay and silty clay textures dom-
inating. Cecil, Madison, Lloyd, Georgeville, and Hudson are the more preva-
lent soils. On the surface, they range from sandy loams to silt loams, with
subsoils ranging as mentioned above. The soils have moderate to rapid external drainage and moderate internal drainage. They are suitable for diversi-
fied agriculture.

For Wilkes County, seventeen soil types and one phase are identified
(Long 1916). These residual soils are derived from crystalline, igneous, and
metamorphic rocks. The county is believed to be underlaid by a basic metamor-
phosed schist (Long 1916:13-14). At the Toombs House, soils belong to the
Cecil series, one of the five soil groupings in the county. The soil on the
surface is classified as Cecil clay loam, a reddish-brown to brownish-red,
friable soil, with an average depth of fifteen to twenty centimeters (Long
1916:21). The transition from the top soil to the subsoil is abrupt. The subsoil is a brick-red or deep-red, densely compacted clay (Long 1916:21). Cecil
clay loam is the most extensive soil type in the county, with practically no
variation of the subsoil (Long 1916:21-2).

Climate

Jedidiah Morse, in his 1797 American Gazetter, described the climate of
the piedmont of Georgia this way:

> From June to September the mercury in Fahrenheit's ther-
> mometer commonly fluctuates from 76. to 90. In winter from
> 40. to 60. (1797:unpaginated).

George White described the weather of Wilkes County thusly: "The climate is

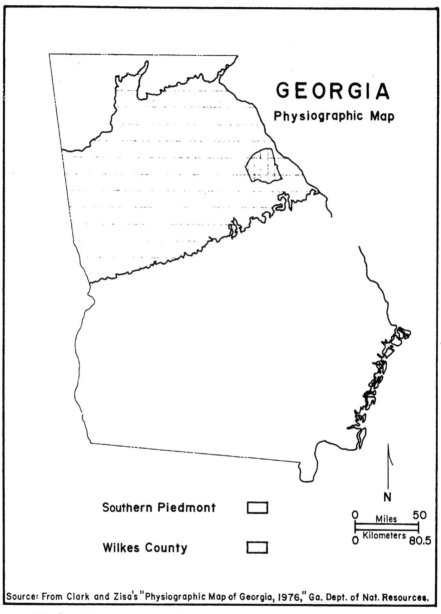

GEORGIA

Physiographic Map

Southern Piedmont ☐

Wilkes County ☐

N

0 ___Miles___ 50

0 Kilometers 80.5

Source: From Clark and Zisa's "Physiographic Map of Georgia, 1976," Ga. Dept. of Nat. Resources.

Fig. 6. Wilkes County in the Southern Piedmont Physiographic Section.

subject to great changes" (1849:609; 1854:681). Long (1916:7) states that the mean winter temperature is 43.1° F. and the mean summer temperature is 78.1° F. The annual mean precipitation is 48.82 inches (121.75 cm), with the least rainfall in autumn (Long 1916:7). In a publication of the U.S. Department of Agriculture, Climate and Man (U.S.D.A. 1941:821), this weather information was collected at a recording station in Washington (no dates are given; see Table 2). These records and observations indicate no dramatic shifts in the climate of Washington from the 1790s to the present.

Vegetation

As a botanist accompanying a team of surveyors and others "appointed . . . to ascertain the boundaries of the new purchase," Bartram observed vegetation during this excursion (1792:34-46). His description is too long to quote, but this trained observer recorded an informative picture of the original Wilkes County area (see Harper 1958, for a map of his route). Morse, in his gazetteer of 1797, reported the forests of Georgia's piedmont consisting of oak, hickory, mulberry, pine, and cedar (1797:unpaginated). More recently, a soil report for Wilkes County states that the native forest on Cecil clay loam was predominantly hardwoods of oak and hickory, with shortleaf and loblolly pine second in abundance (Long 1916:22). Current studies substantiate these earlier reports.

On a broad scale, Kroeber studied cultural and natural environments of North America for the purposes of understanding their relationships and the viability of the concept of "culture area" (1938). To accomplish this monumental task, he drew on the research of appropriate authorities of natural environments. In a summary section on North American vegetative types, Kroeber classifies the piedmont under a subsection of "Deciduous Forest," character-

TABLE 2

WEATHER INFORMATION COLLECTED AT WASHINGTON, GEORGIA

Temperatures and Precipitation

Length of Record	Jan. Aver.	July Aver.	Maximum	Minimum	Annual Precipitation
40 years	45.5° F.	80.5° F.	109° F.	-4° F.	48.67 in.

Killing Frosts

Length of Record	Last in Spring	First in Fall	Length of Growing Season
38 years	March 28	November 8	225 days

izing the area as "Piedmont Deciduous Forest" (1938:17-8). Shelford, a natur-
alist, in discussing deciduous forest regions, classifies an area which includes Wilkes County as "oak-hickory" (1963:18-20, Figure 2-1). Typifying
this forest are post oak, white oak, and black oak (Shelford 1963:57).

More areally specific, Brender states that original upland forest of the
Georgia piedmont was an oak-hickory climax, intermixed with American beech,
red maple, yellow poplar, American chestnut, and a scattering of shortleaf and
loblolly pines (1974:34). He comments that the oak-hickory type reached its
best development on deep, sandy loams overlaying the red clay of Lloyd, Davidson, and Cecil soil series (Brender 1974:34). Historical research has con-
firmed Brender's assertions.

Plummer studied eighteenth-century forests of Georgia by examining the original district survey records, which do not include Wilkes County. Of these
areas surveyed according to the district system, Morgan County environmentally
simulates Wilkes most closely. Morgan County was covered by a forest of oak,
pine, and hickory on Cecil soils (Plummer 1975:9). Plummer elaborates by sta-
ting that those surveys conducted on the piedmont, covering more than a half-
million acres, showed the forest as oak-pine-hickory, with a ratio of 53:23:8
(1975:16). Wharton asserts that the typical "red clay" of the Cecil, Lloyd,
and Davidson soils supported an oak-hickory forest formerly covering fifty to
seventy-five percent of the piedmont uplands (1977:145, 153). Based on this
information, historical and contemporary, observational and analytical, we may
conclude that the forest of the Wilkes County area was predominantly oak, hickory, and pine when Joel Abbot began building a home in Washington, Georgia,
in the 1790's.

Animals

No indepth treatment of fauna, native or imported, will be undertaken

here. A cursory discussion is warranted as a part of environmental setting.
For a sample of the native types, Parmalee's classification of faunal remains
archaeologically recovered from Mound C at Etowah Indian Mounds (9 Br 1) in
Bartow County, Georgia, offers some insight (Van Der Schalie and Parmalee 1960:
48-9). He identified the following, which is not a complete list.

Mammals: whitetail deer; black bear; beaver; opossum; rab-
bit; gray squirrel; fox squirrel; raccoon; marsh
rice rat; mountain lion; canid; bobcat; squirrel;
gray fox; striped skunk

Fishes: freshwater drum; catfish; sucker; redhorse; bass;
walleye

Amphibians: bullfrog

Reptiles: rattlesnake; common box turtle; pond turtle; turtle; snapping turtle; soft-shelled turtle

Birds: turkey; passenger pigeon; Canada goose; sandhill
crane, et al.

Bartram mentioned seeing deer, turkey, elk, rattlesnake, glass snake,
bear, tiger (panther), wolf, wild cat, butterfly, and moth, during his jaunt
through the "new purchase" (Harper 1958:29-30). Some early travelers' accounts record sightings of fauna, but the reliability of the untrained obser-
vers must be considered (see Mereness 1961; Jones 1965; Lane 1973). White includes in his Statistics of the State of Georgia, a "Catalogue of the Fauna
and Flora of the State of Georgia" (1849). The categories covered are mammals,
birds, reptiles, fishes, insects, crustacea, shells, and plants. Unfortunately, little information about distribution is given.

The historical record of fauna is sparse for the Indian-early European
occupancy of Georgia, even for mammals (Golly 1962:11). In addition to the
domestic imports of cow, chicken, pig, and horse by Europeans, we assume the
early settlers adapted to the exploitation of native fauna for subsistence

needs, as well as sport.

Cultural Environment

As preparation for archaeology at the Toombs House began, a question arose about Joel Abbot. Why would a young physician leave Ridgefield, Connecticut, for Washington, a small town on the frontier of Georgia? The question, I eventually realized, was inherent to a contemporary perspective of Washington. The town of today, obviously, is not the Washington of the 1790's. To gain understanding of Abbot's migration, some knowledge was needed of the cultural history of Washington and Wilkes County, and the context in which these political entities originated and developed. This task was undertaken by researching the expansion, settlement, and development of this area of the state. This research was done with the frame of reference of thinking of the area as "frontier." In 1790, Washington was only twenty miles east of the western boundary of Georgia, which bordered Cherokee lands. This boundary, however, was not the only frontier.

Abbot's 1794 arrival in Washington found the town on a number of frontiers. The Revolutionary War had ended only eleven years earlier. Georgia, like the other former colonies, was a new state struggling for recognition while establishing a political identity. The "New Purchase," an Indian cession of about two million acres, had been obtained by the colonial government just before the Revolution began. The first federal census had been conducted in 1790, showing Wilkes County with a population of 31,500 (State of Georgia n.d.:1116). In the largest and most populous county of the state, Washington was not on a frontier (Hawes 1963), but on frontiers. However, the concept of frontier as a term suggesting the outer limits of knowledge or settlement is dubious. Dr. Abbot and the residents of Washington may have been on a variety of frontiers, but one of them was not a dearth of knowledge about the country-side around them. Hitz's article, "The Earliest Settlements in Wilkes County" (1956), is of insufficient time depth and geographical scope to bring contextual clarity to the setting in which Washington originated and developed. We must seek those currents and events which will provide a perspective through which to see the Washington of the 1790's.

Expansion

Perhaps some would expect a subsection on exploration, but the early explorers provided few details about the places they visited in the New World. They brought back to Europe knowledge of a new hemisphere with exotic residents, and inflated prospects of abundant sources of wealth and power. Reports of explorers, however, were written to obtain support for return voyages, and more ships, while providing a minimum of locational information for competitive reasons.

The initial factor resulting in many effects on the piedmont of Georgia was the establishment of the colony of South Carolina in 1670. The foremost city in this settlement was Charleston. Its merchants quickly recognized the value of trade with the Indians (see Crane 1929). Alliances with these neighbors were negotiated for trade with ulterior motives of defense and expansion (Crane 1929:22). Good relations with the Indians protected the infant colony from their threat and those of imperial rivals (Crane 1929:136). After three decades of trading and negotiating, Carolina traders were able to penetrate the interior as far west as the Mississippi River (Crane 1929:46).

The routes over which these Carolina traders traveled existed long before they came (see Myer 1928). Indian paths were from thirty to forty-five centimeters wide (Dunbar 1937:19; Myer 1928:743; Phillips 1908:31), extending to

all parts of the Southeast. This extant, overland network was critical for
the Carolina traders as they moved westward, because the primary drainage systems of the Southeast flowed south to the Atlantic Ocean and Gulf of Mexico
(Crane 1929:23). At the heads of navigation of these drainages, Indian paths
were intersected. These routes generally followed the fall line, where the
rivers were fordable at the rapids and sand bars (Thompson 1954:62). South
Carolina and its traders, however, were not alone in their quest of commercial
success with the native Americans.

South Carolina's borders were exposed to more than powerful groups of
threatening Indians. The western border of the colony met with the commercial
rivalry of France, whose representatives sought Indian alliances as they penetrated the interior of the continent along the Mississippi River (Crane 1929:4;
Newton 1970:136). Carolina's southern border flanked lands claimed by Spain.
The competition was more than commercial rivalry among the European powers; it
was imperial expansion (Crane 1929; DeVorsey 1961; Hudson 1976:435; Ivers 1974).
In this struggle, the traders of Carolina were forced to overcome what appeared
to be a geographical disadvantage.

France and Spain expanded their trade by water. Their primary means of
penetrating the areas of the interior they sought to claim and exploit was by
boat along the coastlines as well as the navigable rivers and streams. The
Carolina traders could use the streams and rivers of the Southeast for only a
short distance from Charleston, as the waters flowed south and the traders
were moving west. The water routes were used, in conjunction with paths, to
the heads of navigation where Indian paths were intersected which led west and
northwest (Crane 1929:129; Thompson 1954:62). To the borders of Florida and
Louisiana and to the mountains, the main paths diverged in eastern Georgia
from their origins near the intersection of the fall line and the Savannah

River (see Figure 7). Geography required Carolina traders to deal directly with terrain and the native inhabitants. Few rivers and streams afforded the chance to bypass areas or Indians in lieu of more favorable conditions. Because of this geographical requisite, Carolina traders rapidly became acquainted with Indians and their environments, providing an asset, primary knowledge of people and geography (Newton 1970:136).

In addition to this requisite of overland travel, Carolina traders had to employ Indians as burdeners for carrying trade goods to the interior as well as the results of exchange back to port (Logan 1859:263; Crane 1929:23; Vassar 1961:406; Weaver 1972:33). Some have suggested that the opening of inland commerce in America has always employed packhorses, but this does not seem to be the case for the Southern colonies (Earle 1900:242; Phillips 1908:31). Forty-eight years after the establishment of the colony, the Board of Trade of South Carolina made this statement:

> Tell the Cherokees we shall hereafter endeavor to ease them of the labor and trouble of carrying burdens. Pack-horses are now being collected to take their places on the trail (Logan 1859:263).

Due to the scarcity of horses, traders had to negotiate with the Indians for laborers, that is, 'burdeners," to transport their trade goods. Thus, because of the necessity of overland travel and of a shortage of horses, Carolina traders quickly accumulated first-hand knowledge of the interior of the country and of its native residents, using an existing network of paths. The country and the Indians located west of the Savannah River were not unknown commodities to the Carolinians. The traders actually served as a reconnaissance force for the settlement phase (Newton 1970:135-6).

Before 1733, the date Georgia was settled, South Carolina constituted the southern British line of defense in the New World against French and Spanish imperialism. To stabilize this boundary, King George I, in 1719, bought South Carolina from its proprietors and made it a royal colony. Subsequently, in 1732, a new colony was established west of the Savannah River. It was named Georgia after King George II, who had aided James Edward Oglethorpe and other English noblemen in undertaking a philanthropic venture. The initial result for South Carolina was to relieve the colony of exposure to French and Spanish intrigue. Georgia was the new buffer for British imperialism in the Southeast (Candler 1937 31:331; Corry 1936:22; Sayer 1942: 19, 21).

With the establishment of the colony of Georgia, changes regarding Indian trade began. The Trustees of the colony and Oglethorpe were acutely aware of the lucrative trade of South Carolina merchants with the Indians. Oglethorpe was determined that Georgia assume jurisdiction over Indian trade within its chartered boundaries (see Candler 1904 1:18; Spalding 1977:29). The preamble of an act passed by the Trustees in 1733 states the following:

> Whereas the Safety Welfare and preservation of the Colony of Georgia doth in great measure depend on the maintaining a good Correspondence and regulating the Trade to be carried on between Your Majesty's Subjects and the several Nations of Indians in Amity with the said Colony . . . (Candler 1904 1:31).

The title of this act reflects the significance which Oglethorpe and the Trustees gave to relations with the native residents of the new colony: "An Act for maintaining the Peace with the Indians in the Province of Georgia" (Candler 1904 1:31). Oglethorpe and the Trustees thrust themselves quickly into negotiating and maintaining relations with the Indian residents and neighbors of the new colony (Candler 1902 2:120).

In 1733, the Trustees appointed Oglethorpe Georgia's commissioner of

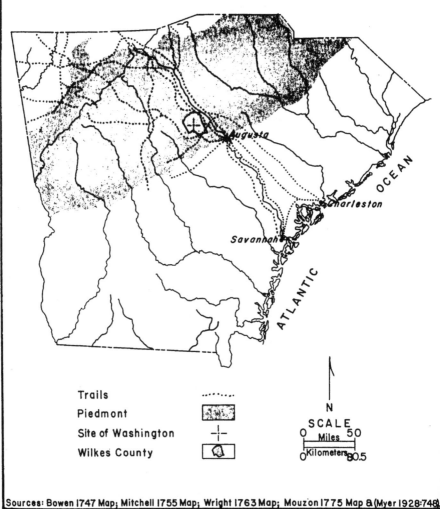

GEORGIA — SOUTH CAROLINA

Colonial Period

Trails from the Coast into the Piedmont

OCEAN

Augusta

Charleston

Savannah

ATLANTIC

Trails ········

Piedmont

Site of Washington ─┼─

Wilkes County

N

SCALE
0   Miles   50
0 Kilometers 80.5

Sources: Bowen 1747 Map; Mitchell 1755 Map; Wright 1763 Map; Mouzon 1775 Map & (Myer 1928:748)

Figure 7.   Georgia - South Carolina: Colonial Period Trails from the Coast into the Piedmont.

Indian trade (Ivers 1974:65). Trade with the Indians was important to the colony, and good trade relations built allegiances in the event of conflict with
France or Spain. For now, the eastern and southern borders of this new colony,
not South Carolina, were subject to threats of imperial rivalry.

Oglethorpe and his officers wasted little time in dealing with Indians
along boundaries which Georgia shared with them. With the Lower Creeks, Oglethorpe negotiated a treaty of trade and peace in May of 1733. Six years later,
at Coweta Town (near present-day Columbus), he negotiated an acknowledgement
of the grant for the colony and definition of its boundaries (see Figure 8),
defined Creek lands, established an alliance against settlement in Creek lands
by Spanish or others, excepting the Trustees of Georgia (White 1854:121).
Oglethorpe was keenly aware of the role of Indians in the success of Georgia's
affairs. He directly sought alliances with the Indians, because he knew the
colony was too weak to ward off any concerted attacks of European rivals either
directly or through manipulations of Georgia's Indian neighbors.

Oglethorpe recognized that controlling Indian trade was more than commercially advantageous, it was defensively imperative for Georgia. By licensing
all traders conducting business in Georgia and specifying towns for each of
them, Oglethorpe attempted to control this trade. Licensing was more than a
commercial objective, because the conduct of traders had drastic effects on
Indian relations with the colony. Traders had often jeopardized relations between the colonial governments and the Indians because alienation of Indians
or untimely war could mean financial loss for themselves (Corkran 1962:11).
South Carolina had refused to assert control over the behavior of the traders
despite numerous complaints by Indian officials (Ivers 1974:5-6). Corry described Indian traders as "dissolute, given to heavy drinking, quarrelsome, law-
less, and quick to take advantage of the ignorance of the Indians in matters

GEORGIA
1739

Georgia of 1739   ▨

N

0   Miles   50

0   Kilometers   80.5

Source: Compiled By De Vorsey (1961:142, Fig. 17).

Fig. 8. Georgia According to the August 1739 Treaty with a Nebulous Western Boundary Defined as "high as the tide flows".

of weights and measures and of skin values" (1936:33). Oglethorpe eventually
won the right to license traders, including those from South Carolina. However, he was never able to wrest from Georgia's colonial neighbor the economic
benefits of Indian trade, most of which flowed to Charleston merchants throughout the colonial period (Ivers 1974:71; Ready 1970:162). South Carolina could
not be pushed too far by Oglethorpe.

Oglethorpe and the colony of Georgia were in an environment which necessi-
tated compromise in order to survive. Serving as a buffer for South Carolina
against the rivalry of France and Spain, Georgia could not act assertively toward its colonial neighbor for fear of alienating a source of needed support
in case of war (Ivers 1974:70). Nor could Georgia act harshly against the Indians who shared so much of the colony's border. Indian allegiance was imperative to Georgia's defense. The colony's conciliatory Indian trade policy
failed. It was not adaptable to the imperial economy of the frontier (Fant
1931:222). This was probably a consequence of the need to compromise in order
to survive. Instead of extracting cessions from the Indians, Oglethorpe acknowledged Indian rights to the resources of the forests (Candler 1904 1:31;
DeVorsey 1961:137). In spite of this commercially inadequate policy, the settlers of Georgia were not ignorant of the interior of the country. Through
the perpetuation of Indian trade, compounded with colonial and imperial rivalry, Georgians had to know the territory and its native residents to survive.

The point of this discussion of Indian trade and colonial settlement is
to elaborate the role of economics in spurring imperial expansion. Carolina
and Georgia traders opened the interior of the Southeast in spite of their in-
tra-colonial rivalry. Using the existing network of Indian paths, the traders
penetrated deeply into the backcountry and the lives of its Indian residents.
The traders rapidly became informants of these unknown lands and peoples. As

Corkran has said of Carolina traders among the Cherokee, the trader's reports, "be they rumor or grim truth, formed the fibers from which colony and crown wove the fabric of their Indian policies" (1962:11). These men who lived astride shifting imperial claims, commercial rivalries, and vacilating Indian allegiances knew their customers and the land in which they lived very well. Not only was this knowledge an economic necessity to the traders, it was an imperative for their physical survival. The area of Georgia which eventually became Wilkes County was not unknown territory. It was frontier in the sense of lacking British political control and settlement.

Spain, France, and Britain were obviously imperial and commercial rivals in the New World, each attempting to establish permanent settlements through which to extract the riches of this vast, unknown land. In addition to colonial bases through which to manipulate the Indians, these competitors sought fortunes and resources to supplement their own economies. For the Southeast, Charleston traders discovered the value of deer skins in the world markets, especially England's (Corry 1936:40; Crane 1929:115). Vast quantities of deer skins were traded by the Indians for European manufactured goods brought by the Carolina traders. New ways of life were brought to the Indians by trade, while fostering a dependence on the European society of the traders (Corry 1936:33; Crane 1929:116-7; DeVorsey 1961:11-13; Hudson 1976:435-43; Ivers 1974: 5; Swanton 1946:741-2; Wilms 1973:19). Stuart, Indian superintendent for the British Southern department for fifteen years, characterized the relationship this way:

> The original great tie between the Indians and Europeans was mutual conveniency. This alone could at first have induced the Indians to receive white people differing so much from themselves into their country. . . . A modern Indian cannot subsist without Europeans; and would handle a flint ax or any other rude utensil used by his ancestors very

> awkwardly; so what was only conveniency at first is now become necessity and the original tie strengthened (DeVorsey 1961:12).

From a historical point of view, the imperialistic significance of Indian trade conducted by the Europeans outweighed the trade's commercial advantages. For Britain and the Southeastern Indians, the excellence of British trade goods counterbalanced the superior position and diplomacy of the Spanish and French (Crane 1929:115). Once a demand for merchandise not manufactured by Indians was created, control of Indian allegiance became a matter of manipulating the flow of European trade goods. By extending credit and supplying firearms and ammunition to the Indians, British traders subverted Indian economies, making themselves more than economically necessary to the Indians (Hudson 1976:436). The Indians became dependent on the traders for their subsistence (Swanton 1946:741-2).

British traders not only were the bulwark of imperial expansion into Indian lands, but sources of information about the interior of the Southeast. As they returned to their ports, traders spoke of the quality and quantity of land to the west of the colonies. This information served only to build causes for colonial expansion, whetting desires of kings as well as migrants and speculators for plenty of cheap land containing abundant resources.

Settlement

European settlement of Georgia began as a coastal venture with the establishment of Savannah in 1733. Under the Trustees, a body of twenty-one appointed Englishmen governing from London, the colony grew slowly. James Oglethrope negotiated the settlement of the colony in 1733, with the Lower Creek Indians. In 1739, he defined boundaries for Georgia in a treaty negotiated with Creeks, Cherokees, and Chickasaws (see Figure 8):

> . . . all the lands on the Savannah River, as far as the
> river Ogeechee, and all the lands along the seacoast as far
> as St. John's River, and as high as the tide flowed . . .
> (White 1854:121).

Oglethorpe left Georgia for England the last time in 1743, removing a dynamic
source of leadership for the struggling colony. The Trustees continued their
philanthropic experiment with decreasing success, returning again to Parliament
in 1751 for additional funding to carry on the venture. Parliament denied
funds, and King George II forced the Trustees to surrender their charter. The
colony and charter were turned over to the king in 1752, and, in 1754, a royal
government with a governor was created.

From the original settlement of 152 emigrants, Georgia's population grew
slowly under the Trustees. By the early 1750's, the population was estimated
to be about 3,000 (Coleman 1960:11; DeVorsey 1961:148; Greene and Harrington
1966:181). For a variety of reasons, many of the newcomers to Georgia left
for South Carolina and other colonies. However, after the installation of a
royal government, the colony began to prosper.

In 1758, the General Assembly of Georgia passed an act reorganizing the
colony into parishes. The tidal limit of the 1739 treaty was ignored by this
act, and the Indians were not informed of this consequence (DeVorsey 1961:146).
In this same year, another act was passed prohibiting the private purchase of
land from Indians. This was apparently an attempt to appease Indians complain-
ing of border violations while maintaining governmental control over the acquisition of land. By 1762, Georgia's population increased significantly to
11,300, reflecting peaceful relations with Indians under a stable and respon-
sive government. In 1763, the Spanish surrendered Florida to the British,

while the French extinguished their claims in the Southeast. Freedom from ri-
val European threats and peace with Indians made Georgia inviting to settlers.
At the same time, in the older colonies to the north, events were occurring
which built migrational pressures (DeVorsey 1961:25; Ramsey 1964:17-22).

Northern colonies received daily new emigrants seeking good, cheap land.
As population increased, so did demand. As good land became scarce, the price
of it rose. In addition to the Indians, the mountains on the western margin
of these colonies limited expansion. With the high price of available land,
the scarcity of new land, the growth of population, and the high price of con-
sumer goods, the pressures of migration were having effects for Georgia.
Growth in Georgia was not coming inland from the coast, but from the northeast
(Zelinsky 1951:194-5). The demand for new land was not from new emigrants,
but from migrants from the older colonies (Belcher 1964:2). A direct consequence for the colonial government of Georgia was on relations with Indians.

Between 1752 and 1762, the population of Georgia increased from approxi-
mately 3,000 (Greene and Harrington 1966:181) to about 11,300 (DeVorsey 1961:
148), without a commensurate increase in colonial territory. The problem facing the government was how to encourage growth and prevent disastrous conflict with the Indians as an expanding population encroached on land claimed
by the native residents (DeVorsey 1961:13). In 1763, a congress of governors,
chiefs, and others met at Fort Augusta to discuss problems in light of the removal of French and Spanish threats. A new and "permanent" boundary was delineated between colonial Georgia and the Creek Indians. However, this boundary
was not demarcated until 1768 (see Figure 9). During this interval, the migration of settlers to Georgia was unceasing, and reproduction by residents was
unfaltering (DeVorsey (1961:157). An estimate of 18,000 residents in Georgia
is made for 1766 (Belcher 1964:2). Legislation encouraging settlement was

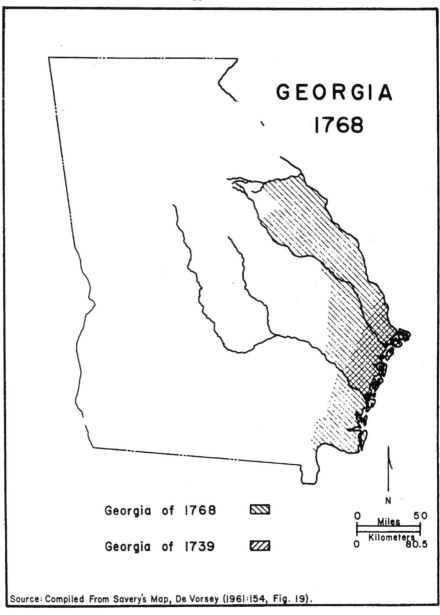

GEORGIA
1768

Georgia of 1768   ▨

Georgia of 1739   ▨

N

0   Miles   5.0

0   Kilometers   80.5

Source: Compiled From Savery's Map, De Vorsey (1961:154, Fig. 19).

Fig. 9.   Georgia According to the Treaty of 1763 Delineation and 1768 Demarcation.

enacted this same year. By 1769, the governor of Georgia had to issue a pro-
clamation ordering the removal of settlers from Indian lands as defined by the
1768 boundary. Nevertheless, the additional acreage demarcated in 1768 was
not the end of the struggle for land. New pressures were building. As pay-
ment for debts, estimated to be as much as 45,000 pounds for the Cherokees
alone, traders were persuading Indians to convey land to them (Hitz 1956:8-9).

In 1773, the governor of Georgia negotiated a cession from the Cherokees
and Creeks, the "New Purchase," in exchange for the abolishment of debts in-
curred by the Indians from the traders (Bartram 1792:33; for discussion, see
Corry 1936:28; Crane 1929:166-7; DeVorsey 1961:170-2; Hitz 1956:8-9; Ivers
1974:5-6; see Figure 10). This cession added two million acres to the colony.
Further cessions were delayed by the Revolutionary War.

During the war for independence, Georgians adopted a state constitution
in 1777. From the parishes and cessions which had made up the colony, the cre-
ation of counties was authorized. Article IV of the constitution states that
"the ceded lands north of the Ogeechee River shall be one county, and known by
the name of Wilkes (see Figure 11; McElreath 1912:230-1; Watkins and Watkins
1800:8-16); the remainder was divided into seven other counties.

In 1790, two events occurred which affected the original Wilkes County
boundary. One, a treaty was negotiated between the United States government
and the Creek Nation, with the Indians ceding land between the Ogeechee and
Oconee rivers (Kappler 1904 2:25-9). Two, out of Wilkes County, the state legislature began creating new counties. In 1790, Elbert County was created entirely from Wilkes; by 1800, all or part of Oglethorpe, Warren, and Lincoln
counties were partitioned from Wilkes by the legislature (see Figure 12; Bryant 1977). Again in 1825, Wilkes lost land when Taliaferro County was created
(see Figure 13). Figure 12 portrays the political boundaries Joel Abbot would

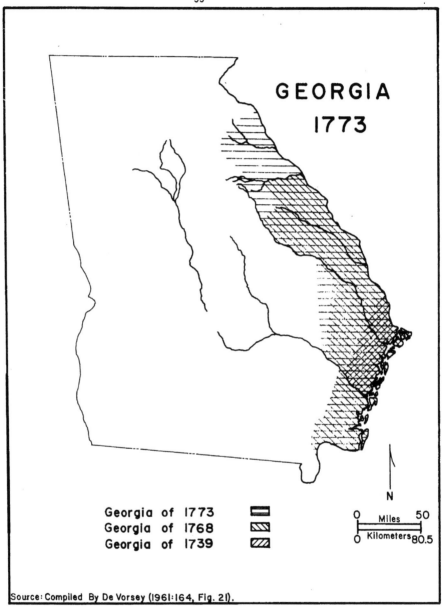

GEORGIA
1773

Georgia of 1773
Georgia of 1768
Georgia of 1739

N

0   Miles   50

0   Kilometers 80.5

Source: Compiled By De Vorsey (1961:164, Fig. 21).

Fig. 10. Georgia According to the Survey and Demarcation of the 1773 "New Purchase."

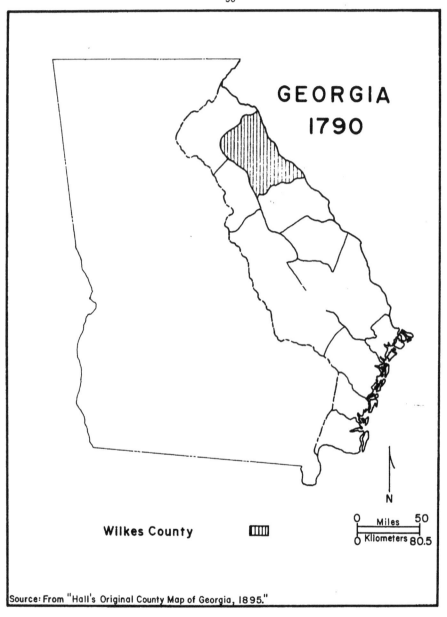

GEORGIA
1790

Wilkes County

N

Fig. 11. Wilkes County as Established in the Georgia Constitution of 5 February 1777.

GEORGIA
1800
New Counties

Counties Created From Wilkes Co., 1790-1800.
Wilkes Co.

Elbert Co., 1790
Oglethorpe Co., 1793
Warren Co., 1793
Lincoln Co., 1796

0   Miles   50
0   Kilometers   80.5

N

Source: From "Hall's Original County Map of Georgia, 1895."

Fig. 12. New Counties Created From Wilkes County Between 1790 and 1800.

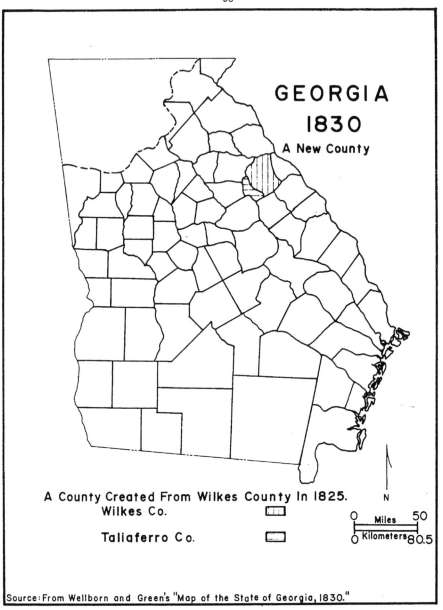

GEORGIA
1830
A New County

A County Created From Wilkes County In 1825.
Wilkes Co.

Taliaferro Co.

N

O   Miles   50

O   Kilometers 80.5

Source: From Wellborn and Green's "Map of the State of Georgia, 1830."

Fig. 13. Taliaferro County Created From A Part of Wilkes County In 1825.

have known when he arrived in Washington in 1794.

After a slow beginning under the Trustees, the rate of settlement of Georgia rose under a stable royal government (Tarver 1968:5). Excluding the war years, this trend continued. Abbot's migration to Washington in 1794 was merely another statistic of the growth of Georgia's population. A relatively peaceful environment and abundant, cheap land were irresistible inducements to settlers.

Development

As we have already discussed, the penetration of the interior of the continent by explorers, and more thoroughly, by Carolina and Georgia traders, was by means of an existing network of Indian paths. To understand development on the Georgia piedmont and on the frontier(s) to which Joel Abbot migrated, consideration of this network is warranted.

> In the earliest days the trading paths were merely aboriginal thoroughfares which the Indians or traders traveled with human loads of skins and trade goods. They next became traces for pack horse trains. Then, as the Indians gradually moved west, the whites took possession of the familiar paths through the wilderness and made them in to crude pioneer roads (Weaver 1972:33).

The routes and means by which people and goods move into an area is crucial to any understanding of development.

Routes, that is, paths, to the interior for conducting Indian trade were no doubt maintained by the traders (Phillips 1908:31). The early phase of this trade, as mentioned, used "burdeners." A consequence for the path network was probably little more than some deepening by the wear of increasing traffic and load. Some widening may have occurred due to more passings and meetings. Also, routes may have been altered to meet changing commercial and

military needs and priorities of Indians and traders. However, the path network was probably not drastically affected until the common use of the horse
as a means of transportation. Beasts of burden brought new requirements to the
path network. An examination of these developments and their consequences
tells us much about Washington and Wilkes County.

An early map of the "new purchase" shows no paths in the vicinity of the
area which was to become Washington (see Figure 5). Of course, the route of
every path existing in the cession at that time may not be recorded on the map.
Certainly, though, those paths significant to commerce and warfare were. Another early map, "A New and Accurate Map of the Province of Georgia in North
America" (1779), identifies the land between the Little and Broad rivers as
"Hunting Grounds of the Cherakees [sic] and Muskohgees" (see Figure 14). The
Indian path network in this area probably had a subsistence priority rather
than one of commerce or warfare. By 1796, Carey's map portrays an extensive
network of "roads" across eastern Georgia (see Figure 15). Maps, nevertheless,
may lead one to make false assumptions if interpreted as documents of fact
(DeVorsey 1971; Schuyler 1977:100-01). Features identified as roads were often
nothing more than paths (Phillips 1908:167).

Some of these early paths, often called by such names as "trades,"
"tracts," "runs," and sometimes "roads" (Goff 1956:219), were vividly described
in accounts of travelers. Featherstonhaugh (1847 2:219), spoke of an area of
Georgia "without any roads, but obscure Indian trails almost hidden by the
shrubs and high grass." Another traveler in the new America made this observation: "I always found the roads, or rather the paths, bordered and obscurred
[sic] by copse or forest . . ." (Volney 1804:6). McCall, an early Georgia his-
torian, reported 'a path was opened to Savannah from Augusta which was passable
by horseback" (1784:34). The road was "formed apparently by the mere removal

61

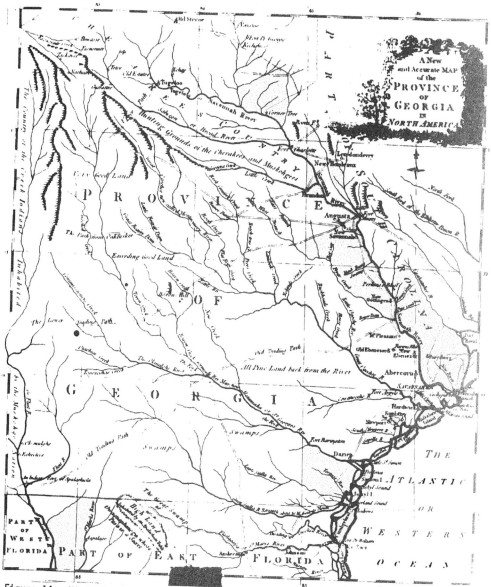

Figure 14.   Hinton's 1779 Map of Georgia Identifying the Area of Washington-Wilkes County as "Hunting Grounds of the Cherakees and Muskohgees" (Surveyor General Department, Office of the Secretary of State, Atlanta).

Figure 15. A Portion of Carey's 1796 Map of Georgia Clearly Showing Washington (Surveyor General Department, Office of the Secretary of State, Atlanta).

of the requisite number of trees to open a path through the forest" (Buckingham 1842 1:188). These brief comments indicate the problem of applying the
term "road" to corridors of early travel in Georgia.

Dramatic effects for the Indian-trader path network came with the use of
the horse. Traders replaced burdeners with horses. The path network endured
hooves as well as feet, and more weight, more frequently. With the addition
of the horse, a new set of problems arose. Traders began assembling packhorse
trains as horses became plentiful (Phillips 1908:31); these trains were often
combined into caravans. A single caravan may have consisted of a hundred
horses, each bearing 150 to 200 pounds of goods, accompanied by fifteen or sixteen persons (Rights 1931:409; Rothrock 1929:14; Vassar 1961:406). Such in-
creases in numbers, weight, and probably frequency as demand grew, must have
taken a toll on the original path network. In addition, horses created other
problems as their needs were not the same as those of the Indian burdeners or
the traders.

The problems brought by horses had consequences for the path network beyond accelerated wear. Indians who may have lived along paths used by the traders seldom grew extra grain to sell or trade. This unavailability of a commercial source of feed affected the path network. To secure feed, traders
probably had to alter some or all of their routes. Goff makes these observations regarding packhorse trains, food, and route selection.

> For wayfarers with a large number of horses, such as the
> Indian traders' packhorse train, it was essential to arrange
> periodic stops at spots where canebrakes could be found. As
> a result of this practice, it is reasonable to conclude that
> the availability of cane along the way was one factor which
> influenced the location of great arterial trading paths . . .
> (1956:218).

There can be little doubt that natural sources of forage were sought by traders,

for they certainly did not want to expend space and horses carrying grain and
fodder.

A number of primary accounts make references to cane, canebrakes, and
their availability to packhorse trains and other consumers. In a 1776 publication, Thomas Pownall, in discussing Georgia, stated: "In other swamps which
are marshy no Tree or Shrub but Fresh-water Marsh, Grass, wild oates & Southward, a Species of Cane, grow; these are said to be good for Horses & Cattle"
(1776:92). Another traveler, as he rode through the Georgia piedmont, made
this comment: "Our Horses met with most delightful tender virgin Cane" (Pope
1792:71). Benjamin Hawkins made references to the availability of cane and
moss in the Creek country (1848:19, 40, 45). At one point, he referred to the
streams above the fall line, "all of them with cane or moss" (Hawkins 1848:20).
Adding to the significance of the wide distribution of the occurrence of cane
is the fact that it is a deciduous plant, offering perennial forage.

Based on the assumptions listed below, the suggestion is made that the
path network found and modified by the Carolina and Georgia traders was not
one comprised of routes along ridges.

1. Little or no forage would have been available for the horses on the
    ridges, at least a portion of the year.

2. Traders wished not to expend space or horses transporting grain and
    fodder in lieu of trade goods and skins.

3. Few water sources would have occurred on ridges.

4. Ridges would have exposed travelers to undesirable climatic and social
    elements (hostile Indians and imperial competitors).

5. Occasional routings over or along ridges probably occurred for pur-
    poses of communication, observation, and expedition.

Obviously, the path network of the packhorse trains did not follow along streams and rivers in the valley bottoms. These waterways did not flow in the direction the traders were traveling in many cases. For Wilkes County, this is not wholly the case, as at least on the return from the interior, traders could float items received in exchanges downstream to Augusta or Savannah. On the whole, though, for smaller unnavigable streams, routing along the banks would have been futile in the Georgia piedmont. Crossing the numerous tributaries would have been arduous and consumptive. Paths were routed or modified to take advantage of those natural features affording rapid, safe travel, and food. Some of these features were fords, canebrakes, moss, gaps, ridge crests, firm soils, and moderate gradients. We suggest that most of the path routes in the piedmont of Wilkes County were situated above valley bottoms on moderate slopes of ridges. A route would be far enough up a slope where tributaries were easily crossed by horses, avoiding dense floodplain vegetation, occasional floods, and soft soils, but accessible to forage, water, and game. Also, it would be far enough below ridge crests to minimize exposure to undesirable climatic and social elements, but accessible to ridges for purposes of observation, communication, and expedition. The frequently made assertion that present highway or railroad systems duplicate the networks of prehistoric Indian paths is unacceptable (Logan 1859:326; Suddeth, et al. 1966:28; Thompson 1950:89; Jeane 1974:37; History Group 1980).

Paths shown on the map of the "new purchase" certainly follow streams and rivers, but back from them (see Figure 5). No paths follow along ridges. Some, however, do intersect them, crossing from one watershed to another. For the historic period in Wilkes County, the road network which developed did not duplicate the one of Indian paths, even though the latter may have been modified by traders using packhorses. By the time the "new purchase" was mapped, many packhorse trains had crossed this area traveling to Cherokee country.

The point of this discussion is to convey a picture of the development of routes over which migrants traveled into the piedmont of Georgia. Most of these routes were merely products of trader traffic widening Indian paths. Euro-American settlers migrated to the Georgia piedmont over a network of modified Indian paths which were nothing more than the product of foot and horse traffic. The history of the development of the piedmont does not finish at this stage; it requires further examination.

During the colonial period, Georgia experienced little improvement of its network of roads and horse paths. The first wagon roads in the state connected Savannah with satellite communities (Coleman 1976:135). Horseback was the common mode of transportation. Bonner states that as late as 1806, the road from Savannah to Darien was in very poor condition. The stage went to Darien, at which point mail, freight, and passengers traveled southward by sea (Bonner 1964:48-9). The coast had many protected shallow waterways over which to travel safely (Phillips 1905:435). This inexpensive alternative no doubt impeded the development of a good highway system along the coast.

On the piedmont in this period, other variables played roles in retarding the improvement of overland transportation. Variables of topography and natural resources affect the organization of settlers; hence, controlling in large measure the demand for and development of a system of transportation (Green 1938:119). For the Georgia piedmont of the 1770's, certain external pressures began to build. Small-scale farmers in Virginia and the Carolinas, pressured by the daily arrival of immigrants seeking land, by decreasing productivity of their own lands, by scarcity of new land, and by escalating prices of goods, sought new opportunities (Callaway 1948:61-2). With cessions of Indian territory and liberal settlement policies, Georgia, as mentioned previously, became subject to migration from colonies to the north and east.

Settlement in the Wilkes County piedmont was made by farm families intend-
ing to produce all which they might need. Some were squatters establishing an
economy of self-sufficiency in isolation from the rest of the world (Newton
1970:136-7; Phillips 1908:50). Others were law-abiding citizens seeking a better life (History Group 1980:3.1.3.). All sought a landscape similar to that
which they had left, so that they could continue the farming practices they
knew (Newton 1974). These migrants, therefore, moved westwardly along those
temperature zones, soil types, and topography familiar to them (Owsley 1945:
168, 174). As small, self-sufficient farmers, these migrants made no demands
for internal improvements. The routes over which they had gained access to
the newly ceded lands apparently met their needs (Newton 1970:138). With the
exceptions of the Savannah and Ogeechee river valleys and the coastal area,
Georgia was devoid of wagon roads prior to 1776 (Weaver 1972:107). Nevertheless, economic changes subsequently affected these isolated, self-sufficient
farmers who had settled the Wilkes County piedmont.

Many of the early settlers of Wilkes County, coming from Virginia, brought
with them knowledge of tobacco farming (Callaway 1948:72). After experimenting
with the soils of their new lands, the settlers found them sufficient for growing tobacco. By 1785, tobacco production had become a major industry of the
Wilkes County area, reaching European markets in relatively large quantities
(Bonner 1964:49). Tobacco farming, however, was unsuited for the large-scale
planter, as it required so much attention (Gates 1960:102). A single laborer
could handle only three or four acres (Callaway 1948:89). Nevertheless, as
the first cash crop of the upcountry, tobacco was grown by almost every farmer
migrating into recent Indian cessions. As tobacco became the chief money crop,
warehouses for its inspection were established at Petersburg, Augusta, and other
towns (Bonner 1964:50; Coleman 1976:110-11; Coulter 1965). The success of a

staple cash crop and the necessity of its inspection resulted in a dramatic change for the upcountry. The economy of self-sufficiency rapidly altered to one dependent on external markets and goods (Green 1938:122). An adequate network of roads for the conduct of commerce became an economic necessity. Something more than horse paths was required.

To the warehouses built at or near heads of navigation on major streams of the Savannah River watershed, the problem for the farmers was getting tobacco to them efficiently. As the number of migrants grew, the opportunity for every farmer to have access to a navigable stream lessened (Green 1938:121-2; Phillips 1905:435). Economic needs, manifested as demands by farmers for internal improvements, focused on the road system. Not until 1786 was any state action taken, at which time the state lay the responsibility of altering public roads or opening new roads on the superior court of each county (Watkins and Watkins 1800:499). Prior to this, roads had been improved by communities in response to local economic priorities; for example, transporting tobacco to inspection warehouses and markets.

A technique of transporting tobacco probably had great effects on the road system. Tobacco was packed into large barrels called hogsheads, capable of holding 1,200 to 1,500 pounds (Gates 1960:103). Often, these hogsheads were tipped over on their sides and equipped in such a way that they could be rolled to an inspection warehouse or market, pulled by a horse (Coulter 1965:107; King 1875 2:635). Tobacco, however, cannot be permitted to get wet, for moisture will damage it. Roads over which hogsheads were rolled had to be dry, with bridges and ferries for crossing streams and rivers. Ridges, therefore, became a desirable topographic feature on which to develop a road system (Bonner 1964: 50; Coulter 1960:251, 1965:23). Thus, "rolling tobacco" to a dock on a navigable stream or along a road to an inspection warehouse resulted in the development of a network of routes which met economic needs -- the most critical of which was the expeditious delivery of a dry crop. Bonner stated that this strategy is the source of the phrase "tobacco road" (1964:50). This change of economics had a significant consequence for the upcountry.

With the establishment of tobacco as a cash crop, the early settlers farming in Wilkes County created new needs. Tobacco had to be delivered dry and in quantity. The network of overland roads had to be wider and drier than a path for a horse. Developing and maintaining an adequate road system became an economic necessity. Success of this crop resulted in another need.

As more farmers turned to tobacco, their heritage of self-sufficiency and independence faded. Cultivating tobacco consumed much of their time. Farmers were no longer able to meet their own subsistence needs and turned to outside markets. Cash obtained in the sale of tobacco was available for the purchase of goods and food stuffs they no longer produced. The road network, therefore, became a corridor over which was transported goods and merchandise for sale to farmers. Finally, as mentioned, with the high rate of settlement, not everyone could obtain land adjacent to a navigable stream. An alternative to boating produce to market had to be developed or improved by those who were landlocked. A system of roads on high ground, namely ridges, disregarding the priorities of traders and self-sufficient farmers, was a response to an economic change. Efficiently getting a salable crop, one which was dry, to market and purchasing items no longer produced became top priorities. A system of "ridge" roads made achieving those priorities possible. Other factors soon came into play which reinforced demands for better overland routes to market.

In addition to the demands of farmers comprising a significant economic voice for internal improvements, new forms of pressure developed. Indian cessions to the west continued across the piedmont. Cessions of 1783 and 1790

opened large tracts west and northwest of Wilkes County for settlement. The
hopes and aspirations of migrants for more cheap, rich land were refueled.
Land in the east which had been mismanaged was abandoned. In 1793, Thomas
Jefferson gave this perspective: "We can buy an acre of new land cheaper than
we can manure an old acre . . ." (Gates 1960:101). Migration pressures were
unabated, and demands for goods and services increased. New land and more migrants were not the only factors involved.

Within twenty years after tobacco had become the principal cash crop, cotton supplanted it (Callaway 1948:72). Green seed cotton had been grown on the
piedmont by the mid-1790's, but due to the tenacity with which the lint clung
to the seed, manually separating them was unprofitable (Bonner 1964:52; Callaway 1948:90). That which was grown was mostly for domestic use. With Whit-
ney's invention, as much as fifty pounds could be cleaned a day as opposed to
a pound manually separated. Cotton, being less difficult to grow than tobacco,
rapidly became the principal cash crop of the piedmont. Its abundant, cheap
production, combined with technological improvements in processing the fiber,
permitted the substitution of cotton fabrics for woolens and linens (Gates
1960:7-8). Gates states that between 1790 and 1815, the demand for cotton resulted in a sixtyfold increase in its production (1960:7-8). Cotton planting
rapidly became the principal activity of planters and farmers seeking to "reap
the profits which high prices and swiftly accelerating demand assured them"
(Gates 1960:8).

As production increased, the needs for internal improvements were voiced
as demands. Even though the outer edge of the "cotton belt" could be reached
by means of navigable streams, an adequate system of overland transportation
within the belt was lacking (Green 1938:121; Phillips 1905:435). The problem
was one of readily connecting the prosperous farmers of the cotton belt with

markets for selling their crop and purchasing food and supplies in return
(Green 1938:122-3; Phillips 1905:435; Weaver 1972:95). Bonner states that, by
1820, two-thirds of the market crops of the piedmont were grown within five
miles of some navigable river, and much of the remainder within ten miles of
some watercourse (1964:54-5). To further develop, therefore, the economy of
the upper piedmont had to have a network of good roads.

In 1796, Tennessee became a state. The westward thrust north of Georgia
had logistical consequences for the Georgia piedmont and Cherokee lands. For
example, a settlement at Ross's Landing, near Chattanooga, established commercial ties across Cherokee land to Georgia. By 1805, the United States negotiated, through a treaty, the use of two roads through "Cherokee country," and
the next year, another treaty granted the right for the movement of mail from
Knoxville to New Orleans (Kappler 1904:83, 84). A treaty in 1816 was negotiated with the Cherokee, giving the United States "the right to lay off, open,
and have the free use of, such road or roads, through any part of the Cherokee
nation . . . as may be deemed necessary for the free intercourse between the
States of Tennessee, and Georgia and the Mississippi Territory" (Kappler 1904:
126). In addition, all rivers and waters in the Cherokee nation were opened
to navigation by the citizens of the United States.

These roads permitted the Cherokee to export surplus products. Nevertheless, they opened the Cherokee nation not only to travelers but to commerce
among its neighbors (Wilms 1973:89). With a federal road connecting Augusta,
Washington, and Athens with Ross's Landing in Tennessee, the commercial success of the upper piedmont was assured (Weaver 1972:98). But as late as the
1820's, even the 1830's, the upper Georgia piedmont lacked an adequate overland
transportation network (Bonner 1964:54-5; Coulter 1965:65-9; Green 1938:123;
Phillips 1905:435, 443; Taylor 1951:24).

This elaborate treatment of the cultural environment warrants a summary discussion. As stated in the opening, the migration of a young physician from Connecticut to a small Georgia town near the western boundary of the state in the 1790's requires cultural-historical context. Without contextual setting, any study of the Toombs House and its residents is insufficient. Too often, when an event or series of related events, such as construction of the Toombs House, is considered, the tendered explanation or cause is ambiguous. This situation is usually the product of insufficient contextual information which might assist in selecting a probable explanation or cause from among possible ones. For Wilkes County, Washington, the Toombs House, and the residents, information about each was available in varying amounts. To assist in assessing the worth of this information and any problems with it, additional indepth research was necessary. This cultural-historical context assisted in identifying and interpreting patterns of cultural behavior manifested in the archaeological record.

Joel Abbot migrated to Washington by routes which were a product of his culture, not that of the native residents. He was a late-comer, traveling with much available information about the country and the Indians. Traders from Charleston and Savannah had preceded him across this portion of Georgia many years before when it was still Indian land. They opened the way for expansion driven by their own commercial interests and backed by colonial governments acting as instruments of imperialistic European rivals. Traders' experiences with the Indians and knowledge of the backcountry not only provided impetus for expansion, but also supplied needed information. As bulwarks of imperial motives, traders, by the nature of their work, reduced the frontier pattern from one of a boundary of knowledge to one of politics.

A consideration of the settlement of Georgia and its patterns aided this

study of the Toombs House. For the Georgia piedmont, the thrust of historic
settlement was not from the coast, nor were the settlers European immigrants.
It was from colonies -- in Abbot's time, states -- to the east and north of
Georgia whose Euro-American residents were migrating. At first, settlement
was slow, but with a change in the form and policies of the colonial government
of Georgia, migration increased rapidly. Indian cessions provided space, while
liberal settlement policies gave incentive. Factors outside of Georgia, such
as hostile Indians, topography, costs of goods and land, and immigration, drove
migrants to the Georgia piedmont in great numbers. They sought new land and
opportunities, both of which were abundant in Georgia. Joel Abbot's migration
to Georgia, therefore, was not exceptional. It was merely a product of socio-
cultural pressures which began building in the older colonies before the Revolutionary War.

Access to the Georgia piedmont for Euro-Americans was initially by an existing network of paths established by the Indians. This network, however,
was modified by Euro-American settlers to meet their own military and commercial priorities. For understanding Washington's founding and growth, this is
important. This town did not grow up beside a major path of Indian commerce
or defense. Its original citing was based on Euro-American military priorities
for the purpose of defense (Bowen 1950:7; Writers' Program of the W.P.A. 1941:
13; Willingham 1969:13). The need for good roads, however, during the settlement phase, was of a low priority. As the piedmont developed, its economy
changed from one based on self-sufficiency to one dependent on commerce. With
this change came demands of residents for internal improvements, which included
good roads.

During the phase of development, the many streams and rivers of the piedmont served as the primary means to reach markets and ports. As the number of

migrants increased, access to waterways became a problem. There simply was not enough waterfront property for everyone. Overland routes of good quality became an economic necessity. This situation was made more critical with the introduction of tobacco and cotton. Farmers were supplying fewer of their own needs and growing staple crops. Roads became imperative to the economy for the conduct of commerce. For example, tobacco had to arrive at market dry, requiring that roads be located on high ground, which, in the piedmont, meant ridges. Washington's location on a ridge crest between two rivers was ideal. The prosperity of Washington was assured because the town was topographically situated astride a corridor of commerce in the development of the piedmont.

Joel Abbot's migration to Washington was not as pioneering as it might first appear. He traveled along well-established routes, and knowledge of the area to which he was migrating was readily available. Washington was not located on the fringes of civilization, but was a prospering community situated in the economic mainstream of the Georgia piedmont. To understand the Toombs House, one must be familiar with cultural-historical context in which it was built and changed.

CHAPTER 4

METHODS, TECHNIQUES, AND DATA REQUIREMENTS

Working hypotheses were generated in response to problems encountered and refined by historical and architectural research of the Toombs House. They influenced the selection of methods and techniques while delineating data requirements. The hypotheses will be examined regarding the needs and sources of data as well as the means of data recovery. With this approach, the working hypotheses may be separated into two sets. This is based on the nature of the problems which the hypotheses address as well as the data requirements of the hypotheses. After a cursory look at the hypotheses and their consequences for methods, techniques and data requirements, a discussion of selection and of techniques follows.

The Working Hypotheses

The working hypotheses are separated into two sets. The first set is composed of problems of phases of construction, dates of these phases, and season of construction of each phase. The second set is the problems of removal of appendages and relocation of the house.

Set One

Hypotheses

Hypothesis for construction of the house in phases (No. 1):

The Toombs House was constructed in four temporally distinct phases.
Hypothesis for the sequence of phases of construction (No. 2):

Room A-4/5/6/7 was constructed first; Room A-9/10, second; Room A-1/2, third; and Room A-8, fourth.

Hypothesis concerning the season of construction of footings and foundations (No. 5):

The form and placement of a footing trench relative to the footing contained may indicate the season in which the foundation was constructed.

Data Needs

1. Vertical sequence of footing trenches, footings, and foundations.

2. Juxtaposition of footing trenches, footing, and foundations of phases of construction.

3. Chronologically diagnostic artifacts.

4. Sealed contexts for artifacts, etc., e.g., footing trenches undisturbed.

5. Diagnostic building materials.

6. Diagnostic building techniques.

7. Dimensions of footing trenches relative to the positioning of footings in the trenches.

Data Sources

1. Footing trenches.

2. Footings and foundations.

3. Features associated with footing trenches.

4. Artifacts from footing trenches or associated features.

Data Recovery Techniques

1. Observation.

2. Excavation.

3. Recording.

4. Screening.

5. Collecting.

6. Informal analysis.

Set Two

Hypotheses

Hypothesis for the removal of appendages (No. 3):

Prior to the construction of Room A-1/2, an appendage was attached to the east side of Room A-4/5/6.

Hypothesis for the relocation of the house or some portion of it (No. 4):

The Abbot portion of the Toombs House, Room A-4/5/6/7, was moved south from East Robert Toombs Avenue.

Data Needs

1. Remnants of structural features of the former appendage.

2. Evidence of activities associated with the removed appendage.

3. Features indicative of a house being moved.

4. Remnants or evidence of previous activities on the present site of the house.

5. Circumstantial historic evidence.

6. Temporally diagnostic artifacts.

Data Sources

1. Footing trenches, footings, foundations, postholes, posts, drip lines, etc., as remnants of former appendage.

2. Trenches, footing, and foundation anomalies.

3. Treadways, walkways, wells, landscaping features.

4. Diagnostic artifacts.

5. Historical sources.

Data Recovery Techniques

1. Observation.

2. Excavation.

3. Recording.

4. Screening.

5. Informal analysis.

6. Analysis of historical data.

Subject and Problem Selection

Selecting a subject through which to investigate a problem, or set of problems, was not a segment of this project. The subject, the Toombs House, was a given, resulting from State acquisition. Selecting an appropriate method of investigation, archaeology, and techniques was a response addressing problems discerned by other forms of research and of the nature of the resources thought to be pertinent to these problems. The problems to be investigated were the results of architectural and historical research. As resources subject to these lines of inquiry were exhausted, alternatives were sought. Resources beneath the surface of the ground in the basement of the Toombs House were acknowledged as holding potential solutions. Archaeology was recognized as the appropriate method for investigating these subsurface resources.

Complete investigation of the archaeological resources of the basement was unfeasible due to limitations previously discussed. Only a sample of the resources, therefore, could be investigated. The entire surface of the ground in the basement was accessible, as all framed flooring was removed for restorative purposes. The selection of areas for archaeological investigation was judgmental. Four factors formed the basis of this selection. First was the set of unsolved problems discerned by preceding research. Second was an assessment of the archaeological potential of the basement founded on preparatory research. Third was the arrangement and condition of architectural features of the basement. Fourth was objectives of restoration and interpretation of the house. Those areas of the basement judged to be most productive in meeting the informational needs as defined by problems of restoration, interpretation, and research were archaeologically investigated. Other areas were treated as additional needs of information arose. The methods and techniques employed are a consequence of selecting those appropriate to meet the needs of the investigation and the resources.

Means of Data Recovery

Techniques of data recovery were those of standard archaeological practice. For the field phase, selection was guided, of course, by the problems under investigation, by priorities of restoration, by theoretical assumptions, and by the working hypotheses. Some elaboration of the techniques used follows.

To objectively control space, two techniques insured consistency of reference to location, as well as research (all preceding work used the U.S. Customary System of measurement). Based on the U.S. Customary System, a benchmark was established, and a grid was imposed on the basement area. For control of vertical space, a benchmark, or arbitrary datum, was set on a concrete boundary marker at a low elevation on the Toombs House property (see Figure 16). The mark served as a point of reference for vertical measurements; that is, all elevations of the basement were so many inches, feet, etc., above this spot. Because of the distance of the arbitrary datum from the house, an interim datum was established on the sill of the door in the south wall of Room 4/5/6 (see Figure 16). This point was 24.74 feet above the arbitrary datum of zero at the concrete boundary marker. All subsequent elevations were taken relative to the interim datum point.

For control of horizontal space, a cardinally oriented grid was imposed on each space investigated. The grid provided a network of perpendicularly intersecting lines to which all horizontal measurements referred; that is, a point was so many inches, feet, etc., east and north of lines of the grid. All references to portions of horizontal space were measured east and north of the southwest corner of the specific unit under investigation.

Control of time was afforded by the technique of excavating according to observable stratigraphy of the basement. As the top stratum, or layer, of soil was excavated, it was assumed to have been the most recently deposited. Subsequent layers of soil were accordingly excavated, each assumed to be older than the layer previously removed above it. This procedure continued until culturally sterile soil was reached. All artifacts and records were associated with the layer of soil from which they came or to which they pertained. Elevations of layers of soil, artifacts, and features were recorded in reference to the interim datum point, providing a sequence of vertical relationships in space.

All units were excavated manually with shovels, spades, trowels, spoons, or other instruments permitting the scale of recovery appropriate to the resource. Size of a unit was judgmental, based on needs of data recovery (problems), on architectural parameters, and on personal convenience. A variable

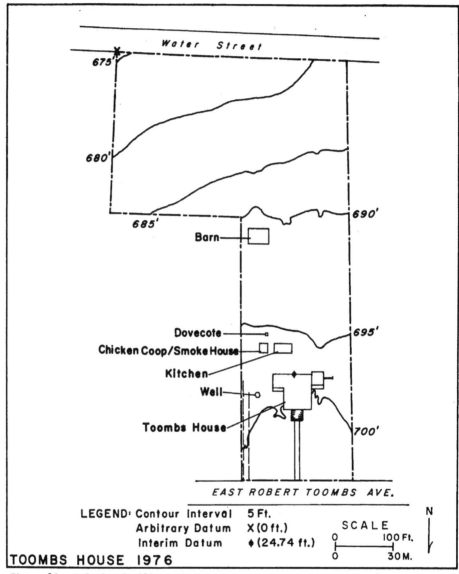

Figure 16. Existing Facilities and Contour Map of the Toombs House Property - 1981.

affecting the size and placement of a unit was the availability of light. Working in the enclosure of the basement under artificial lighting required adjustments to obtain adequate visibility. Procedural flexibility was a requisite for meeting unfamiliar conditions of the basement.

All excavated fill was sifted manually through hardware cloth. Size of cloth opening changed during the course of investigation due to soil conditions and excavation objectives. Size ranged from one-quarter-inch to one-half-inch openings. All artifacts recovered were bagged according to layer and unit of recovery.

Justification

Use of the method of archaeology at the Toombs House is justified on two accounts. One, preceding architectural and historical research resulted in some problems to which solutions were inconclusive. Resources other than those subject to these lines of inquiry were sought. Other resources, hopefully, would contain solutions, or at least indications of solutions. The archaeological potential of the Toombs House was acknowledged as an untapped resource worthy of investigation. Two, this new resource, an archaeological one, was to be subjected to restorative activities, regardless of its potential or integrity. In the context of unsolved problems and of imminent loss, appropriate investigation of this resource was warranted. Archaeology was the appropriate method for retrieving data from this resource in a scientific manner.

The use of South's Mean Ceramic Dating Formula (MCOE) is appropriate in this investigation for two reasons (1972). First, as the Toombs House is not an archaeological resource in its entirety, a technique of ceramic analysis more refined than absence-presence was seen as a necessity in this context. Change through time and space was potentially very subtle. Components for analysis were the various phases of construction of the house, each phase a unit of comparison. The MCDF offers the potential of dealing with these potentially subtle frames of reference.

Second, the utility of a new technique of analysis such as the MCDF can be tested only by its application to problems. Only then is the opportunity for refinement or failure given. The hypothesized sequence and phases of construction of the Toombs House offer opportunities to test the method and its applicability to new conditions.

Curation

All artifacts, photographs, plats, maps, notes, and other records are curated at the Laboratory of Archaeology, West Georgia College, Carrollton.

CHAPTER 5

ANALYSIS

To review for beginning this section on analysis, architectural and historical research of the Toombs House generated a number of problems for which offered solutions were tentative at best. Some of these problems were critical for interpreting the house. During the review of restoration plans and specifications, some proposed measures were assessed as having a destructive potential for resources pertinent to interpretive problems. Archaeology was the appropriate means to retrieve information from those resources subject to restoration. Archaeology, therefore, entered the preservation strategy for the Toombs House. Its goal was to assist in solving interpretive problems while mitigating the effects of restorative measures on resources in the basement.

In addition to attacking some problems generated by other forms of investigation, preparatory research for archaeology generated a problem. It pertained to footing trenches and their dimensions, and to footings and their placement in trenches. Relevant information was readily accessible as informational needs of this problem coincided with those of the other problems being investigated.

This first section starts with a discussion of the problems and their refinement for archaeology. This is followed by a treatment of each problem in the context of its working hypothesis and test implications. Data for each test implication are presented with appropriate discussion. Data requirements and sources, as well as techniques of recovery, were outlined in a previous section (see "Methods, Techniques, and Data Requirements") and will be

- 84 -

addressed only if specific needs arise.

Problems, Hypotheses, and Test Implications

For archaeology at the Toombs House, five problems were addressed. Previous non-archaeological research of the house identified four problems; these concerned phases of construction, sequences of these phases, removal of appendages, and relocation of the house. For archaeology, these problems were refined as follows:

1. The house is a product of more than a single phase of construction, but how many is uncertain.

2. The probable sequence of construction of architecturally and historically identified phases is A-4/5/6/7 (Abbot portion) first, A-9/10 (north wing) second, A-8 (west wing) third, and A-1/2 (east wing) fourth.

3. Historical research indicates an appendage of the Abbot portion (A-4/5/6/7) was detached and moved to another property; architectural research discovered features indicative of appendages removed from the east and north sides of the Abbot portion.

4. Historical research found evidence suggesting the Abbot portion may have been moved, i.e., relocated.

The fifth problem, generated by preparatory research for archaeology, does not focus solely on the Toombs House. It promotes study on a more general level of research. The subject is determining the season in which foundations were constructed.

5. Can placement and dimensions of a footing trench relative to a footing reflect the season in which the trench was dug and the footing was laid?

These problems directed archaeology, but hypotheses were necessary to define informational needs. A working hypothesis for each problem was generated. Each hypothesis is presented in an order corresponding to that of the problems. Then, in terms of test implications derived from each hypothesis, the respective problem is analyzed.

Problem 1

For the first problem concerning the number of phases in which the Toombs House was constructed, four temporally distinct phases were hypothesized. Architectural and historical research delineated phases based on style and form of the frame of the house (see Figure 17). Restoration plans prescribed repairing and waterproofing all foundations. For additional information about the number of phases, junctures of the foundations of each phase were assessed as having the highest data potential. These factors combined to focus archaeology on foundations. Undisturbed footing trenches, their contents and associated features, were assessed as the primary sources of information.

Hypothesis: The Toombs House was constructed in four temporally distinct phases.

From this hypothesis, five test implications were derived. Each will be examined.

Test Implication 1: The configurations of footing trenches and associated features will delineate phases of construction.

This implication is based on the assumption that the event of original construction at this site, or consequences of this event, namely footing trenches, will be affected by subsequent construction, that is, built over, modified, or removed. If space A-4/5/6 is the oldest portion of the house, then

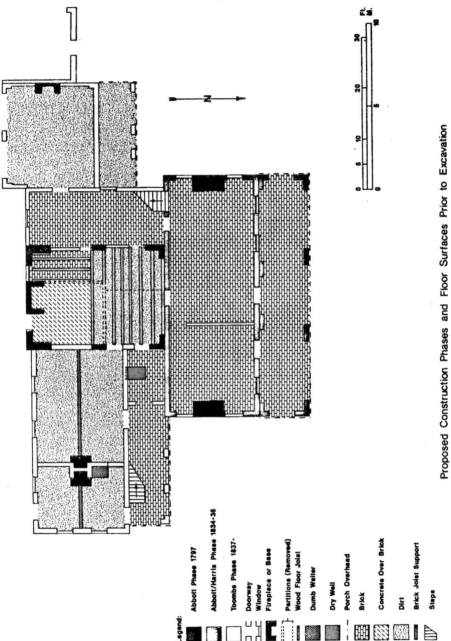

Legend:

Abbott Phase 1797

Abbott/Harris Phase 1834-36

Toombs Phase 1837-

Doorway

Window

Fireplace or Base

Partitions (Removed)

Wood Floor Joist

Dumb Walter

Dry Well

Porch Overhead

Brick

Concrete Over Brick

Dirt

Brick Joist Support

Steps

Proposed Construction Phases and Floor Surfaces Prior to Excavation

Figure 17. A Plan of the Basement Floor of the Toombs House Prior to Archaeology.

subsequent construction should affect in some discernable manner footing trenches and associated features of this space. Points along foundations at which such effects would most likely occur were at junctures of phases of construction. Junctions of phases of framing proposed by architectural and historical research were extrapolated down to the foundations of the house. These points were the focus of investigation (see Figure 18). Of fourteen junctions extrapolated, eight were investigated. Of these, five are discussed and illustrated.

Effects of subsequent construction were assessed to manifest themselves in a number of ways on the configuration of footing trenches and associated features. Pertinent variables which were used to distinguish phases of construction were trench integrity (present, modified, absent), configuration (width and depth), and continuum (continuous, discontinuous). Figures 19 through 23 indicate that the footing trenches of space A-4/5/6 were affected by subsequent construction of additional portions of the house.

In Figure 19, the proposition of juncture is supported by two factors of trench configuration. First, the profiles of the trenches are dissimilar. The trench of the pier is narrower and shallower than that of the east wall. The face of the trench of the east wall is sloping, while that of the pier is nearly vertical. Second, the trenches are physically discontinuous. In Figure 20, trench configurations indicate juncture on the basis of two factors, profile and integrity. The trench of the pier is wider than the one for the wall, and it is slightly shallower. The integrity of the east face of the trench of the pier is modified in this case, interrupted by the trench of the wall.

Juncture is indicated in Figure 21 by two factors, configuration and

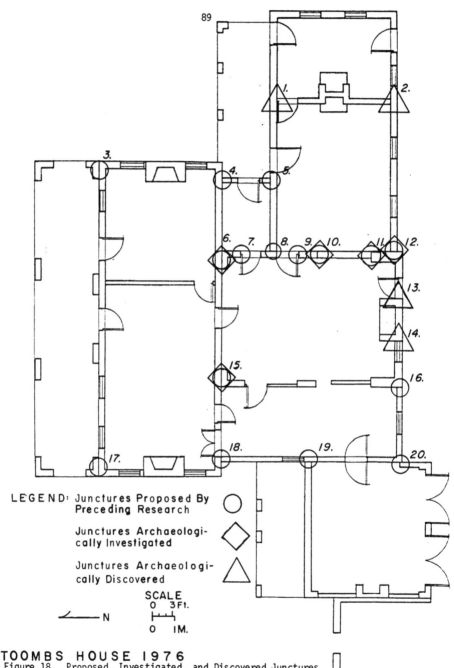

89

LEGEND: Junctures Proposed By
        Preceding Research

Junctures Archaeologi-
cally Investigated

Junctures Archaeologi-
cally Discovered

SCALE
0   3Ft.

0   1M.

N

TOOMBS HOUSE 1976
Figure 18.   Proposed, Investigated, and Discovered Junctures
      of Foundations at the Toombs House.

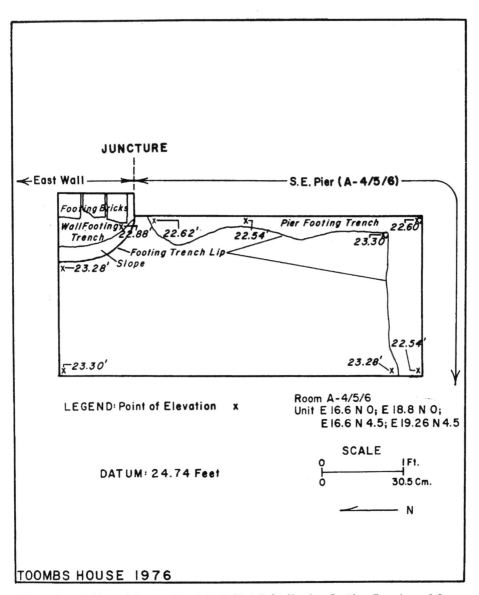

JUNCTURE

←East Wall —————→|←———————— S.E. Pier (A-4/5/6) ————————

Footing Bricks

Wall Footing
Trench — 22.88' X 22.62'   X 22.54'   Pier Footing Trench   22.60'

23.30'

Footing Trench Lip

X—23.28' Slope

22.54'

X—23.30'   23.28'

LEGEND: Point of Elevation   x

Room A-4/5/6
Unit E 16.6 N 0; E 18.8 N 0;
         E 16.6 N 4.5; E 19.26 N 4.5

DATUM: 24.74 Feet

SCALE

0 ——————————— 1 Ft.
0 ——————————— 30.5 Cm.

←————— N

TOOMBS HOUSE 1976

Figure 19.   A Plat of Excavation Unit E 16.6 N 0, Showing Footing Trenches of Room A-4/5/6.

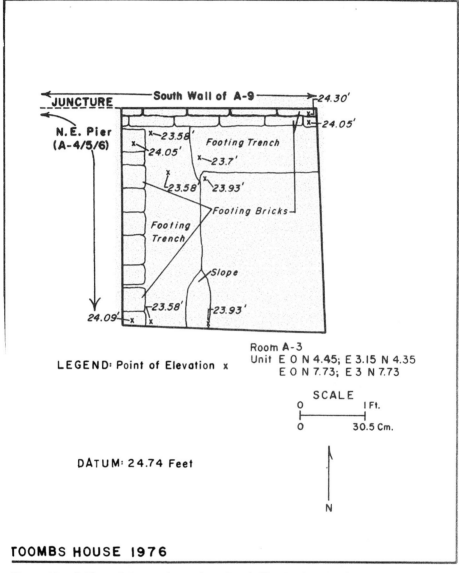

LEGEND: Point of Elevation x

Room A-3
Unit E O N 4.45; E 3.15 N 4.35
E O N 7.73; E 3 N 7.73

SCALE

DATUM: 24.74 Feet

TOOMBS HOUSE 1976

Figure 20.   A Plat of Excavation Unit E O N 4.45, Showing Footing Trenches of Rooms
A-4/5/6 and A-9.

continuum. The trench of the pier is deeper and narrower than the trench of the east wall. The continuum of the trench is interrupted, suggesting a source of change, namely juncture.

For the northwest pier of A-4/5/6, footing trench configurations indicate juncture by two factors (see Figure 22). The footing trench of the wall modifies the integrity of the footing trench of the pier by interruption. The easternmost face of the footing trench of the pier is absent, removed by the digging of the trench for the wall. The trench profiles differ in that the trench of the pier is narrower, shallower, and its face steeper than the trench of the south wall.

The exterior of the southeast pier of A-4/5/6 exhibits a footing trench affected by two subsequent constructions (see Figure 23). The north end of the pier trench is affected by the construction of the east wall and the south end by the wall of A-2. This point has been treated from the interior, or west, side (see Figure 19). However, the configuration of the pier trench is affected by two factors. The profile of the pier trench is deeper and wider than that of the trench of the east wall. The trench of the east wall modifies the northern face of the pier trench by interruption. As for the south wall of A-2, pier trench configuration manifests two factors of effect. The integrity of the eastern face of the footing trench of the pier is interrupted by the footing trench of the south wall. The profile of the pier trench is wider and deeper than that of the south wall trench. In this case, however, the point of juncture is not indicated directly by the contrasting configurations of the trenches. The trench dug for the south wall as it extended westward toward the pier interrupted the footing trench of the pier and simply incorporated it.

Other points of juncture indicated by preceding research were not investigated for various reasons. Points 16 and 18 exhibited·on the surface of the

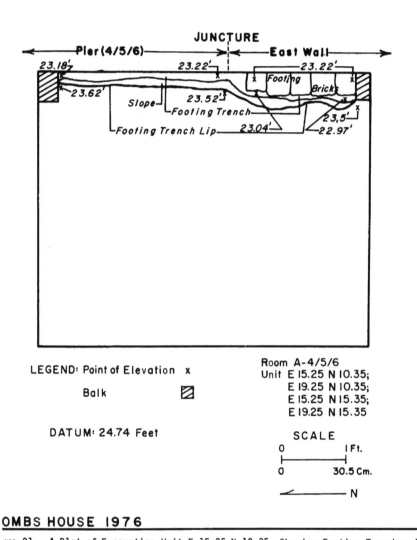

JUNCTURE

←————— Pier (4/5/6) —————→|←——— East Wall ——→

23.18'
23.62'
Slope
23.22'
23.52'
Footing Trench
Footing Trench Lip
23.04'
Footing
Bricks
23.22'
23.5'
22.97'

LEGEND: Point of Elevation x

Balk

DATUM: 24.74 Feet

Room A-4/5/6
Unit E 15.25 N 10.35;
E 19.25 N 10.35;
E 15.25 N 15.35;
E 19.25 N 15.35

SCALE
0   1 Ft.
0   30.5 Cm.

←————— N

OMBS HOUSE 1976

ure 21. A Plat of Excavation Unit E 15.25 N 10.35, Showing Footing Trenches in Room A-4/5/6.

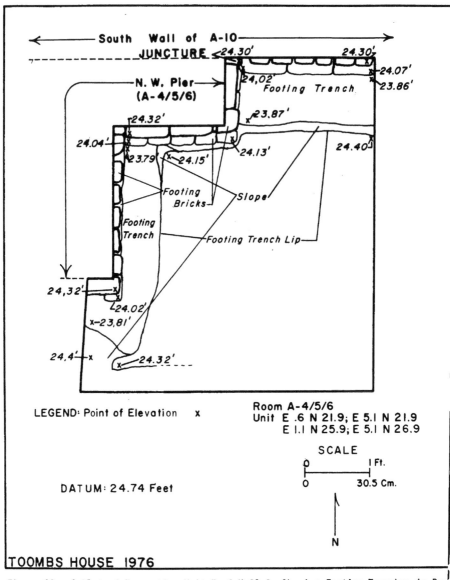

Figure 22. A Plat of Excavation Unit E .6 N 21.9, Showing Footing Trenches in Roo
A-4/5/6 and A-10.

95

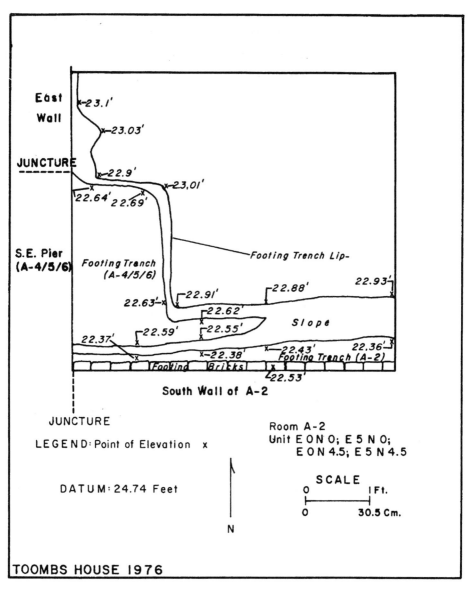

Figure 23. A Plat of Excavation Unit E O N O, Showing Footing Trenches of Rooms A-4/5/6 and A-2.

ground sources of disturbance, while points 3 and 17 were not critical to the purpose of this archaeology (see Figure 18). Given the limitations of time and money, the decision was made not to investigate these. Point 19, however, was investigated, but footing trenches at this proposed juncture were not discernable. Considering the clarity which other footing trenches had exhibited, the assumption of disturbance was made. The source of disturbance was not identified.

Test Implication 2: Foundations of each phase of construction are composed of distinctive building materials.

All of the foundations of the house which were above ground level and observable were built of brick. Many of the surfaces of these foundations had been altered by deterioration and replacement, while interior surfaces had been plastered, stuccoed, or painted. Undisturbed or unaltered exposure of many of these surfaces was unavilable. Excavation revealed that all were of the same material as above ground level. Surfaces of these portions of the foundations, however, were undisturbed by deterioration, replacement, or coverings. The criterion of brick size, therefore, might be a variable which could be treated on these undisturbed surfaces. Observations and measurements could be made readily and collected.

No formal procedure of selecting bricks for measurement was implemented. Sufficient exposure of footings and foundations by excavation permitted visual comparison of surfaces in selecting brick to be measured. Measurements were collected according to the phases of construction proposed by preceding research. Obviously, bricks were not removed from foundations. Forms of brick bonding included headers and stretchers, which exposed all edges necessary for comparison and measurement. Frequently, measurements were compilations.

The edge of one brick, for example, the length of a stretcher, had to be combined with another, the width of a header. These combinations, of course, were made for brick in proximity. Brick archaeologically removed from a footing trench of a particular foundation were also measured and included in this analysis. Other techniques of analysis, such as mortar and brick composition, would have supplemented this superficial effort. Funding, however, was not available. Figure 24 summarizes the observations as recorded in measurements of brick of each proposed phase of construction.

Test Implication 3: Building practices of each phase of construction are distinguishable from other phases.

The implication of this test is that foundations of different phases of construction will exhibit distinctiveness based on contrasting building practices. For brick, the most readily constrasting practice is that of bonding. Brick may be laid in a variety of arrangements, all of which are to prevent the occurrence of laying one brick directly on top of another, that is, stacking (see Moxon 1703:260; Seakins and Smith 1965:33-4). Various arrangements of bonding have been developed during the history of brick masonry. All serve to tie the brick together to form a cohesive mass. These arrangements of brick exhibit patterns which are referred to as bonds (see McKee 1973:49, 51; Ray 1961:120-9; Stoddard 1946:24-5). The assumption is made that once a bond (pattern) is selected by a mason for a foundation, the use of another bond will not occur. Analysis of bonding will treat the foundations according to the phases proposed by architectural and historical research.

Foundations - Room A-1/2. Beginning with Room A-1/2, which is assumed to be a single phase of construction, the following bonding was found. A foundation wall twelve inches wide rested on a footing comprised of a single course of headers in two rows. Centered on this sixteen-inch-wide footing is a row of stretchers on the exterior and a row of headers on the interior (see Figure 25). The result is referred to as a "stepped" footing; that is, the footing extends beyond the face of the foundation wall (Kidder and Parker 1956:172; Moxon 1703:255). The next three courses are laid in common bond.

The arrangement of the row inside the wall is assumed, as no exposure of it was available. The pattern shown is a standard one for a twelve-inch wall laid in common bond (Dalzell and Townsend 1954:29; Graham 1924:304-5; Ray 1961; Seakins and Smith 1965; Stoddard 1946). Interestingly, a footing of two courses is normally recommended for a twelve-inch-wide wall (Dalzell and Townsend 1954:62-3; Godwin 1838:362; Kidder and Parker 1956:234; Stoddard 1946:51-9, 161). However, the framing which this foundation supports is only one story, for which sources recommend only an eight-inch-wide wall (Graham 1924:305; Stoddard 1946:63; U.S. Navy 1972:182). This variance from tradition is unexplained. The twelve-inch width, nevertheless, would maintain continuity of form of foundations, as twelve-inch-wide walls exist throughout Rooms A-4/5/6 and A-9/10, which are thought to be older.

Room A-3. The foundations exposed by excavation in Room A-3 belong to walls of other spaces (see Figure 17). They will be treated under the appropriate room designation to which they belong.

Room A-4/5/6. In this room, a problem arises. The form of foundations is not uniform. Of the six masonry piers of A-4/5/6, the two on the south end are wider than the others. However, the two middle piers are rectangular in form, while the four corner piers are L-shaped (see Figure 17). The discussion begins with the wider L-shaped piers on the south end of A-4/5/6.

The piers supporting the south end of A-4/5/6 are proximate to the fireplace, which may explain their greater width. Due to the mass and consequent

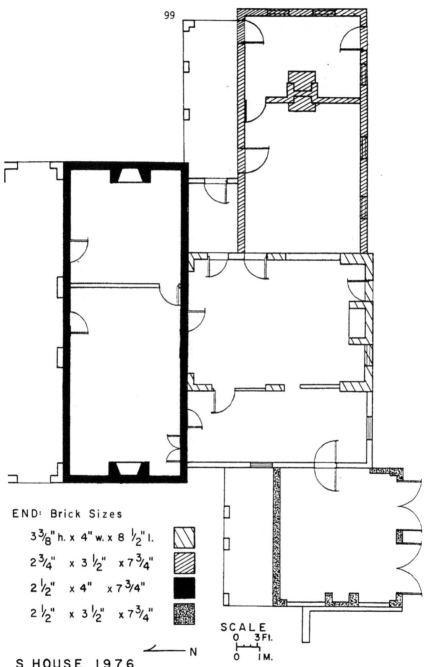

99

END: Brick Sizes

$3\frac{3}{8}$" h. x 4" w. x $8\frac{1}{2}$" l.

$2\frac{3}{4}$"   x $3\frac{1}{2}$"   x $7\frac{3}{4}$"

$2\frac{1}{2}$"   x 4"   x $7\frac{3}{4}$"

$2\frac{1}{2}$"   x $3\frac{1}{2}$"   x $7\frac{3}{4}$"

SCALE

0   3Ft.

0   IM.

N

S HOUSE 1976

4. Measurements of Brick from Proposed Phases of
   House Construction.

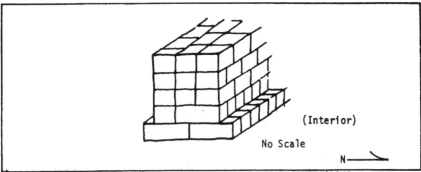

Figure 25. Sketch of Cross-Section of South Wall of Room A-1/2.

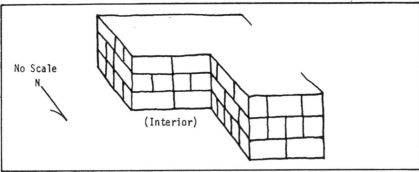

Figure 26. Sketch of Southwest Pier of Room A-4/5/6.

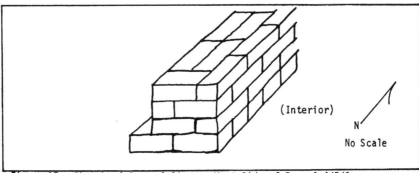

Figure 27. Sketch of Central Pier on West Side of Room A-4/5/6.

weight of the fireplaces and chimney, which serve the basement and two stories above, a foundation of sufficient mass to support the load is required. Adjacent piers may have been built wider to maintain continuity of form with the fireplace. These piers are sixteen inches wide. In none of the units of excavation around them were any "stepped" footings found. This absence is not surprising, as a sixteen-inch-wide pier is more than normally prescribed for supporting a two-story structure (Graham 1924:305).

These wider piers have a standard pattern of bonding. Observations of this bonding were made only on excavated exposures of the outside of the piers. The pattern of bonding exhibited is probably one of the following: "Old English" or "English Cross" (see Dalzell and Townsend 1954:67; see Figure 26). The former is probably the pattern, as it is found on the piers of the north end of A-4/5/6 (see Figure 28) as well.

Piers located centrally on the east and west sides of A-4/5/6 are twelve inches wide. Each is set on a footing of a single course of two rows of headers. The twelve-inch width of the pier is situated asymmetrically of the footings, leaving a four-inch step on the exterior of A-4/5/6. The interior face of each pier is flush with the footing of headers. The arrangement of the inside of the piers is assumed (see Figure 27), but based on known patterns.

On the north end of A-4/5/6, the piers are twelve inches wide and L-shaped. The bonding of footings is different from that of the central piers but similar to the bonding of the southern piers of A-4/5/6. Two courses comprise the footings, with the bottom one being all stretchers laid north-south. The second course of the footing is stretchers laid east-west. This bonding is called "Old English" (Dalzell and Townsend 1954:67). Centrally positioned on this two-course footing is a twelve-inch-wide pier laid in common bond (see Figure 28).

102

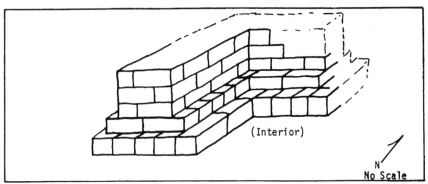

Figure 28.   Sketch of Northwest Pier of Room A-4/5/6.

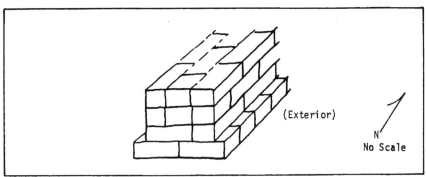

Figure 29.   Sketch of Cross-Section of Wall Between Southeast and Central
Piers on the East Side of Room A-4/5/6.

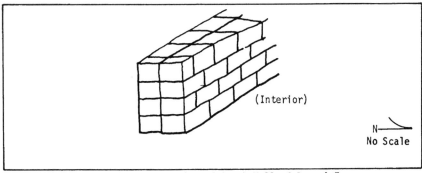

Figure 30.   Sketch of Cross-Section of South Wall of Room A-7.

In addition to the piers of A-4/5/6, there is a masonry wall in this room
to be considered. On the east side of the A-4/5/6, between the central and
southern piers, is a wall of contrasting bond. A twelve-inch-wide wall rests
in the middle of a footing of a single course of a double row of headers, like
the pattern of bonding of A-1/2 (see Figure 25). This leaves a two-inch step,
as the footing is sixteen inches wide. The bonding of the wall is common (see
Figure 29).

Room A-7. Room A-7 is interpreted as the area beneath a porch of the
Abbot portion of the house (A-4/5/6/7). With the Abbot house facing west, this
room would be under a front porch. Only the south and west walls are considered as belonging to A-7. The east wall belongs to A-4/5/6 and the north wall
to A-10 (see Figure 17).

The south and west foundations of A-7 are both eight-inch-wide walls. A
single unit of excavation was opened on the interior of the south wall, but
none on the exterior. Due to historic disturbance, the area on the exterior
was assessed as likely to be one of low return of data for the expenditure of
recovery time. Other exposures were obtained on the west wall. The foundations of A-7 had no stepped footings, that is, courses extending beyond the
foundation wall supported.

Bonding of the south wall began with course of a double row of stretchers
overlaid in common bond for several courses (see Figure 30). The west wall dif-
fers in that interior and exterior exposures disclosed that the bottom course
was headers overlaid in common bond (see Figure 31). The absence of a course of
headers at the bottom of the south wall is apparently a consequence of topographic change (to be discussed later).

Room A-8. Room A-8 has a limited amount of foundation wall (see Figure
17). On the east side is the west wall of A-7. The south wall has two large
bays comprising more than seventy percent of its area. The west wall has two

bays subsequently filled in by construction of the greenhouse. The north wall offered what appeared to be the only unaltered segment. It is twelve inches wide, having a double stepped footing of two courses (see Figure 32). The bottom course of the footing is two rows of headers separated by a row of stretchers, having a total width of twenty inches. The next course, a row of headers flanked by two rows of stretchers, is sixteen inches wide and centrally situated on the bottom course. This gives a two-inch step on each side. The third course, the bottom of the foundation wall, is a row of headers beside a row of stretchers, totaling twelve inches in width. This course is in the middle of the preceding one, resulting in a two-inch step on each side. The remaining courses are laid in common bond.

Room A-9/10. Based on architectural and historical research, Room A-9/10 constitutes a single phase of construction. The foundation walls are twelve inches wide resting on a double stepped footing of two courses (see Figure 33). The bottom course is a double row of headers flanked by a row of stretchers. Resting centrally on this twenty-inch-wide course, a second course has a sixteen-inch width comprised of a double row of stretchers beside a row of headers. A wall of common bond is situated in the middle of the second course. The pattern inside the wall is assumed, as no exposure was available. It is based on a traditional arrangement of bonding of twelve-inch walls (Dalzell and Townsend 1954:29).

Piers and Walls. Besides bonding, other building practices distinguished phases of construction in the Toombs House. The form of foundations is a case in point. The Abbot portion of the house (A-4/5/6) rests on masonry piers. The remainder of the house, excepting Room A-8, rests on continuous load-bearing walls (see Figure 17). Room A-8 has both piers and walls. This distinction of foundation form sets A-4/5/6 off from adjacent spaces of construction (A-1/2, A-9/10, and A-7).

105

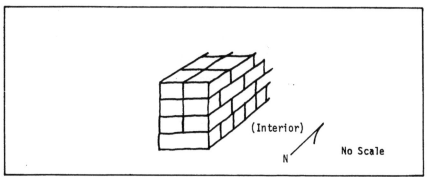

Figure 31. Sketch of Cross-Section of West Wall of Room A-7.

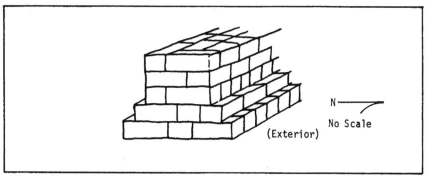

Figure 32. Sketch of Cross-Section of North Wall of Room A-8.

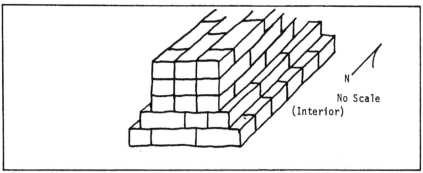

Figure 33. Sketch of Cross-Section of West Wall of Room A-10.

<u>Bonding</u>, <u>Jointing</u>, <u>and</u> <u>Pointing</u>. Some additional observations were made
of building practices exhibited by the foundations. These were made on foundations above ground as well as those exposed by archaeology. The practices in-
volve bonding, jointing, and pointing of brick masonry. As we have seen, the
bonding systems exhibited by footings were informative for discerning phases of
construction. Bonding systems of the walls and piers supported by those footings also were informative. As mentioned, brick are laid in a variety of arrangements of bonding. Two systems of bonding were adopted by the American
colonies from England (McKee 1973:48; Noel Hume 1970:84). They were "English"
and "Flemish" bond. A variation of common English bond called "Liverpool" bond,
which consisted of a course of headers followed by three courses of stretchers,
appeared occasionally in the American colonies (McKee 1973:50). By the nineteenth century, it occurred commonly and was referred to as "American common"
bond. Initially, only four courses of stretchers were used to a course of
headers, but, by 1850, as many as seven courses of stretchers followed a course
of headers (Noel Hume 1970:84). By mid-nineteenth century, the "all-stretcher"
bond became fashionable in the United States (McKee 1973:52). A pattern of
change through time occurs.

No technique of absolute dating is available for analysis of these bonding
patterns. However, one of relative dating is helpful when bonding patterns are
considered in the context of other information. The pattern of American common
bond occurs throughout the foundation walls with the number of courses of
stretchers varying. Table 3 summarizes observations made on the exteriors of
foundation of the Toombs House.

Other observations of building practices included some regarding jointing
and pointing. The former refers to the space between bricks which are filled
with mortar. The latter refers to the treatment of mortar exposed on the

TABLE 3

VARIOUS MASONRY BUILDING PRACTICES
OBSERVED ON FOUNDATIONS ABOVE THE GROUND

Room	Number of Courses of Stretchers Between Headers	Width of Joints (Hundreths of a Foot)	Pointing of Brick Joints
A-1/2	6	.04	Struck without drip
A-4/5/6	4	.05	Flush
A-7	5	.05	Struck without drip
A-8	8	.02-.03	Tooled and scribed
A-9/10	5	.03	Flush

exterior of masonry surfaces. Pointing might result in a particular appearance or in making the exterior of a wall more durable (McKee 1973:70). Widths of joints and techniques of pointing vary in space and time. They are informative in discerning phases of construction (see Table 3) at the Toombs House.

Test Implication 4: Foundations of distinct phases of construction will not be structurally interlocked.

As all of the foundations of the Toombs House are of brick masonry, a phase of construction will be properly bonded, that is, interlocked in such a way that the walls act as a unit in resisting stresses (Dalzell and Townsend 1954; Moxon 1703; Ray 1961; Seakins and Smith 1965; Stoddard 1946). Bricks of one course will overlap those below and will be overlapped by bricks of the course above. In Figure 18, the points at which no bonding, that is, overlapping, existed in footings and foundations exposed by excavation are indicated.

Most of the points at which no form of bonding existed were expected, based on preceding research. A few surprises, however, were exposed during archaeology. In Room A-1/2, the wall which subdivides it (see Figure 17) is freestanding. Prior to restoration, this was unknown, as the walls above the floor framing were plastered, hiding this fact from view. In Room A-4/5/6, the southern piers were found not to be bonded with the fireplace. On the east side of this space, the wall between the central and southeastern piers is freestanding. Unconfirmed archaeologically is the observation that the east wall of Room A-3 is not bonded to the walls it abuts.

Test Implication 5: Dates derived from analysis of ceramics recovered from features resulting from construction, such as footing trenches, will temporally distinguish building phases.

For the house, the primary sources of ceramics for analysis were features

resulting from foundation construction. The primary feature, the footing
trench, was found intact throughout most of the foundations. Only at a few
points was disturbance assumed or evident. When footing trenches or similar
features were encountered in a unit of excavation, they were recorded and excavated separately from the rest of the unit. All materials recovered from
trenches were collected and labeled in association with the feature of origin.
The specific results of analysis for each unit (footing trench, etc.) of collection using South's "Mean Ceramic Date Formula" (1972; 1977) are in the Appendix.
Based on this analysis, results are summarized in a number of tables which follow. From Table 4, discerning phasing according to temporal sequence is difficult. The results have to be further treated. Dates derived from the entire
ceramic assemblage excavated from a particular area have to be separated from
those derived from contexts associated with the construction of that area.
This separation of dates is presented in the following two figures. Table 5
contrasts dates of hypothesized order of rooms with dates or rooms placed in a
temporal sequence. Next, Table 6 shows dates derived by analysis of ceramics
collected from undisturbed features associated with construction of foundations.
The division of some of the areas of the basement was an arbitrary product of
investigation. Now is the time to compare the average dates of total assemblages with those of undisturbed construction features. They are presented in
a temporal sequence to discern any correspondence (see Table 7).

As can be seen, the dates derived from analysis are uninformative for temporally distinguishing phases of construction of the foundations and associated
features. The dates cover a very short temporal range, less than four and one-
half years. Interpretation based on these dates alone is not reliable for distinguishing temporally distinct phases.

TABLE 4

SUMMARY OF DATES FOR VARIOUS AREAS OF CERAMIC COLLECTION
(N/A: Not Appropriate)

Room	A-1	A-2	A-3	A-4/5/6	A-7	A-8	A-9	A-10
No. of ceramics	199	159	45	2,881	1,090	68	37	612
Total ceramic assemblage	1808.2	1810.1	1810.7	1809.9	1807.7	1810.1	1806.4	1806.5
No. of ceramics	3	8	N/A	125	35	14	22	140
Footing trenches	1811.7	1809.6	N/A	1809.3	1804.1	1806.9	1804.5	1808.7
No. of ceramics	5	N/A	N/A	34	N/A	N/A	N/A	N/A
Hearth fill	1809.4	N/A	N/A	1807.0	N/A	N/A	N/A	N/A
No. of ceramics	18	N/A	N/A	N/A	N/A	N/A	N/A	N/A
Construction layer	1807.1	N/A	N/A	N/A	N/A	N/A	N/A	N/A
No. of ceramics	N/A	N/A	N/A	N/A	N/A	N/A	4	70
Joist trenches	N/A	N/A	N/A	N/A	N/A	N/A	1814.7	1806.1

TABLE 5

COMPARISON OF HYPOTHESIZED ORDER OF ROOMS BASED ON PRECEDING RESEARCH
WITH TEMPORAL ORDER OF ROOMS BASED ON DATES DERIVED
BY MEAN CERAMIC DATE FORMULA (MCDF)
(N/A: Not Appropriate)

Hypothesized order of rooms	MCDF date	MCDF date	Temporal order of rooms
A-4/5/6	1809.9	1806.4	A-9
A-7	1807.7	1806.5	A-10
A-9	1806.4	1807.7	A-7
A-10	1806.5	1808.2	A-1
A-1	1808.2	1809.9	A-4/5/6
A-2	1810.1	1810.07	A-8
A-8	1810.07	1810.1	A-2
A-3	N/A	N/A	N/A

TABLE 6

DATES DERIVED BY THE APPLICATION OF THE MEAN CERAMIC DATE FORMULA TO CERAMICS COLLECTED FROM UNDISTURBED CONTEXTS (N/A: Not Appropriate)

Room	A-1	A-2	A-4/5/6	A-7	A-8	A-9	A-10	A-3
Footing trenches	1811.7	1809.6	1809.3	1804.1	1806.9	1804.5	1808.7	N/A
Hearth fill	1809.4	N/A	1807.0	N/A	N/A	N/A	N/A	N/A
Construction layers	1807.1	N/A	N/A	N/A	N/A	N/A	N/A	N/A
Joist trenches	N/A	N/A	N/A	N/A	N/A	1814.7	1806.1	N/A
Average of MCDF dates	1808.1	1809.6	1808.8	1804.1	1806.9	1806.1	1807.9	N/A

TABLE 7

DATES DERIVED BY MEAN CERAMIC DATE FORMULA (MCDF)
FOR PHASES OF CONSTRUCTION IDENTIFIED
BY PRECEDING RESEARCH TEMPORALLY ORDERED

Total Ceramic Assemblage Date (MCDF)	Room Designation	Temporal Sequence	Room Designation	Undisturbed Contexts
1806.5	A-9/10	1	A-8	1806.7
1807.6	A-8	2	A-9/10	1807.7
1809.0	A-1/2	3	A-4/5/6	1808.0
1809.3	A-4/5/6	4	A-1/2	1808.4
1810.7	A-3*	5	N/A**	N/A

*A-3 is included because ceramics were recovered from this area other than foot-
ing trenches.

**N/A = Not Appropriate

Problem 2

The second problem concerns establishing a sequence of construction of the phases identified by architectural and historical research. Based on this research, this hypothesis was generated.

Hypothesis: The sequence of phases of construction is: first, Room A-4/5/6/7; second, Room A-9/10; third, Room A-1/2; and fourth, Room A-8.

Test implications derived from this hypothesis are similar to those for the hypothesis of Problem 1. The results of the test implications will not be repeated but simply referred to or elaborated as dissimilarity necessitates.

Test Implication 1: The configurations of footing trenches and associated features of construction will delineate a sequence.

Configurations of undisturbed features of construction, as previously discussed, did not delineate a sequence of construction for all of the phases hypothesized. For Room A-4/5/6, footing trenches for the foundations were found to be directly affected by subsequent construction of rooms A-1/2 and A-9/10. Evidence of trench integrity, configuration, and continuum indicated that A-4/5/6 preceded A-1/2 and A-9/10 in time.

Test Implication 2: Foundations of each phase of construction are composed of temporally distinctive materials.

All of the foundations of the house were constructed of brick. Unfortunately, observation of the brick permitted a single distinguishing criterion, which was size. Color and hardness are uninformative (Noel Hume 1970:80-1). Even size is not temporally helpful. The problem which arises in attempting to date a structure by its brick sizes is exhibited repeatedly when one measures numerous examples from a foundation only to find a half-dozen different sizes

(Noel Hume 1970:82; Ray 1961:20). Variations of size may be the product of different firings of brick, of different conditions of firing, and of the use of used brick. No materials of construction were found which temporally ordered the phases of construction.

Test Implication 3: Building practices of each phase of construction are temporally distinguishable from other phases.

For the brick foundations, the only temporally distinguishing practice was found in bonding. This practice, however, is only generally informative. In colonial America, two principal bonds were in use: English and Flemish (McKee 1973:50; Noel Hume 1970:84). A new style known as American common bond appeared in the early-nineteenth century, which used four courses of stretchers to every one of headers (McKee 1973:50, 52; Noel Hume 1970:84). About this same time, the "stretcher" or "all-stretcher" bond became fashionable in the United States (McKee 1973:52).

As mentioned in the discussion of "Bonding, Jointing, and Pointing," a change in American common bond occurred through time. The number of courses of stretchers between headers increased. At the Toombs House, a relative sequence is indicated. Room A-4/5/6 has the least number of courses of stretchers between courses of headers. Other identified phases of construction exhibit more courses. The sequence begins with Room A-4/5/6 being the oldest, with four courses of stretchers, followed by Rooms A-7 and A-9/10, having five courses each. Room A-1/2 has six, and Room A-8 has eight courses of stretchers between courses of headers (see Table 3).

Joints, the space between bricks, vary in width for structural as well as aesthetic reasons. Early brick manufacturing failed to produce a unit consistent in size. In order, therefore, to maintain overall uniform dimensions of whatever was being built, a mason used joints wide enough to accommodate variations in sizes of brick (McKee 1973:69). As technology of brick manufacture improved variation is size lessened. With bricks more uniform in size, the width of joints necessary to compensate for variation decreased. Through time, therefore, one should observe a decrease in widths of joints for different phases of brick construction. For the Toombs House, a trend is discernible (see Table 3). Rooms A-4/5/6, A-7, and A-9/10 have the widest joints, five-hundreths of a foot. Room A-1/2 is next at four-hundreths of a foot, and Room A-8 has the narrowest joints. They range from three- to two-hundreths of a foot in width.

Test Implication 4: Dates derived from analysis of ceramics recovered from construction features, such as footing trenches, will temporally order the phases.

Dates derived from the analysis of ceramics by the Mean Ceramic Date Formula were uninformative as to temporal order of the construction of phases. Whether one considers the dates for each analytical unit (A-1, A-2, A-3, etc.) or for each historical/architectural unit (A-1/2, A-3, A-4/5/6/7, A-8, A-9/10), the dates are of insufficient spread to indicate temporal order. Even considering these two perspectives of the basement area, analytical and historical/architectural, in terms of total ceramic assemblages and of ceramic assemblages from undisturbed construction features, temporal order is dubious. Again, the dates are too close together to be informative about order. Dates from ceramic analysis are presented for comparison with dates derived from architectural and historical research (see Table 8).

Problem 3

The third problem is one regarding the removal of appendages. Historical

TABLE 8

COMPARISON OF DATES DERIVED BY VARIOUS MEANS FOR THE HYPOTHESIZED
SEQUENCE OF CONSTRUCTION PHASES IDENTIFIED BY PRECEDING RESEARCH[a]

Phases of construction	Hypothesized sequence of construction	MCDF[b] dates from total ceramic assemblage	MCDF[b] dates from features of construction	Dates from historical research	Dates from architectural research
A-1/2	3	1809.1	1808.4	1865+	1870's
A-4/5/6/7	1	1809.3	1808.0	1797	1790's
A-8	4	1807.6	1806.9	1837+	1870's
A-9/10	2	1806.5	1807.7	ca. 1835	1830's

[a]Thomas 1974; Neal 1981

[b]MCDF: Mean Ceramic Date Formula (South 1972)

research indicates a wing of the Abbot portion of the house was removed to another property (Thomas 1974:100). Architectural research discovered numerous structural indications that a wing was once attached to the east side of Room A-4/5/6, prior to the construction of Room A-1/2 (Neal 1976:Drawings). A hypothesis was formulated.

Hypothesis: Prior to the construction of Room A-1/2, an appendage (wing) was attached to the east side of Room A-4/5/6.

For this hypothesis, three test implications were derived; they will now be treated.

Test Implication 1: Remnants of structural features will be encountered such as footings, piers, foundations, posts, steps, walkways, drip lines, etc.

The area east of Room A-4/5/6, as defined by the walls of Room A-1/2, was examined. The ground within this space was excavated to culturally sterile subsoil. No evidence of features was encountered which could be identified as structural remnants of a former appendage. However, beneath the north wall of Room A-2, the south side of the dry well of Room A-3 was visible (see Figures 17 and 34). Significance of this occurrence is the fact that the wall of A-2 was built over the edge of the dry well, indicating that the well preceded A-2 in time. The north wall of A-2 did not impede use of the well in the past, nor in the present. The existence of the well suggests a set of activities associated with food preparation, conservation, and consumption predating Room A-1/2. Additionally, the highest elevation of sterile subsoil encountered around the top of the well in Room A-3 is almost a foot above the highest elevation of sterile subsoil in Room A-1/2. This difference in elevation may indicate why features of a former appendage east of A-4/5/6 are absent.

Figure 34. Room A-2, North Wall (Interior) Built over South End of Dry Well, Looking North Northeast.

Test Implication 2:   Remnants of construction features will be encountered such
                      as footing trenches, post holes, trash pits, treadways,
                      etc.

   As with the first test implication of this hypothesis, no features remnant
of construction preceding that of Room A-1/2 were identified by archaeology.
Excavation to culturally sterile subsoil encountered only the results of the
construction of Room A-1/2.

Test Implication 3:   Temporally ,diagnostic artifacts associated with construc-
                      tion and structural remnants of the appendage east of Room
                      A-4/5/6 will be recovered.

   In the absence of identified construction and structural remnants of an
appendage to the east side of Room A-4/5/6, no relevant artifacts were recovered in Room A-1/2. Of those recovered, none was analyzed as belonging to any
other period than that represented by A-1/2.

Problem 4

   Some historical research suggests that the Abbot portion (A-4/5/6/7) of
the Toombs House may have been moved back from the road. The implication is
that the road was East Robert Toombs Avenue (Bowen 1950; Thomas 1974; see Figure 16). In Washington, the event of house-moving is not unusual, for today
one can walk through town observing numerous modifications to historic homes,
including visual evidence of moving. The exact reference, "moved back" (Bowen
1950:102), is so vague as to be almost meaningless. In light of this situation,
some preparatory research was conducted. Preceding research provided insufficient information from which to derive test implications for an activity such
as house-moving. What one might expect to archaeologically find as a consequence of moving a house was unknown. The results of preparatory research were

not informative.

No primary sources of the Abbot-house period (1797-1826) were found which pertained to house-moving. In a recent publication, a bibliography listed a number of primary and secondary references (see Curtis 1979), but most, according to their titles, pertain to events of moving rather than to procedures. While attempting to find information from which to generate expectations, another problem surfaced.

Curtis (1979:19-23) discusses three forms of moving a house: intact, partially disassembled, and completely disassembled. For the event at the Toombs House, we have no clues as to the form of the move, if it ever took place, much less the direction or the purpose. Guessing the form is a waste of time. Two forms of moving, intact and completely disassembled, would have very different consequences for the archaeological record. Attempting to formulate expectations of how relocation of a house might manifest itself in the archaeological record seemed almost futile.

Compounding futility was the fact that archaeology was limited to the basement. This meant that not only was the informational basis for the derivation of test implications shallow, but the areal extent of archaeological investigation restricted.

In spite of these problems, a hypothesis was generated.

Hypothesis: A portion of the house, Room A-4/5/6/7 (the Abbot house) was moved
back, i.e., south, from East Robert Toombs Avenue.

The following test implications were derived.

Test Implication 1: Remnants of features resulting from the activity of moving
the house, such as unusually placed trenches, postholes,
pits, treadways, foundations, etc., will be found.

Based on preceding research, the assumption was made that the Abbot portion (A-4/5/6/7) had been relocated, that is, moved south from East Robert
Toombs Avenue. The area north of the Abbot portion, that is, Room A-9/10, was
the focus of investigation. Of course, as archaeology was conducted in other
portions of the basement, evidence of relocation was sought.

No remnants of features indicative of relocation were identified by archaeology. This absence of features, however, does not mean that the house, or
some portion of it, was not moved. The house may have been disassembled and relocated. Also, we may have been looking in the wrong place, as the house may
not have been "moved back" from East Robert Toombs Avenue, but from some other
location in another direction.

Test Implication 2: Anomalous footing trenches, footings, foundations, or associated features resulting from moving the house will be
detected.

Evidence was recovered from foundations which lends support to the idea of
relocation. An attribute of many bricks of foundations exposed by excavation
was that of re-use. Numerous brick had whitewash on them. These whitewashed
brick occurred randomly throughout the foundations of Room A-4/5/6. This was
not an isolated occurrence. In Rooms A-1/2 and A-9/10, whitewashed brick were
observed in foundation walls and joist supports. Painting was not the only
surface treatment observed. In the south wall of Room A-4/5/6, west of the
fireplace, below ground level, a glazed header was observed. A similarly
glazed header was observed in the next-to-the-top course of brick in the chimney on the west end of Room A-10. The random occurrence of whitewashed and
glazed brick indicates only the re-use of materials. The source, or sources,
of these "used" brick is unknown; nevertheless, such materials demonstrate a
former structure. Perhaps the source was the Abbot house at its original

location.

Test Implication 3: Evidence of previous use of the site of the Toombs House.

With investigation restricted to the area of the basement, one source of evidence of relocation might be features indicating previous use of the site of the house. Historical and preparatory archaeological research disclosed no clues regarding uses of the Toombs House site prior to the construction of the Abbot portion (A-4/5/6/7). From the time of the original grant of land to George Walton in 1783, the property which includes the Toombs House site was deeded six times prior to Abbot's purchase (Thomas 1974:54). The price of sixty dollars which Abbot paid for twelve acres suggests his portion was unimproved. Evidence which may conflict with this suggestion of no previous development was discovered in the basement of the Toombs House (see "Unexpected Findings").

During excavation in the northwest corner of Room A-4/5/6, a feature was discovered. Remnants of a foundation were exposed (see Figures 36-38). Details of this feature will be discussed under the section on "Unexpected Findings." The significance is that the Abbot portion of the house was built on the site of another historic structure. The remnants consist of two courses of a brick foundation. The function, form, and period of this feature are unknown except as they relate to the Toombs House. This foundation was the only identified feature indicative of previous use of the site prior to the construction of the Toombs House.

Test Implication 4: Circumstantial historical evidence indicates the relocation of the Abbot portion of the house.

In the absence of substantive evidence of relocation, an examination of historical sources was undertaken. The objective was to ascertain if historic evidence, even though circumstantial, might support an argument of relocation for a portion of the Toombs House. With dates of ceramic analysis clustering in the first decade of the nineteenth century, historical resources of this period were examined. Bowen's only hint to time is as follows: "The house of Dr. Abbot stood nearer to the street than the Toombs House, a portion having been moved back" (1950:102). Direction is inferred to be south, that is, back from East Robert Toombs Avenue. Bowen does not discuss the form or purpose of relocation.

According to a deed, Abbot purchased twelve acres from Williamson in 1797 for sixty dollars on which he was "a building" (Wilkes County, Georgia, Deeds, Book QQ:243). At five dollars an acre, the assumption may be made that the acreage was unimproved (see Thomas 1974:54-66 for comparative information on land prices in Washington). As a matter of fact, the acreage sold to Abbot was a portion of a sixteen-acre tract Williamson had purchased from Stith that same year for $1,000 (Wilkes County, Georgia, Deeds, Book RR:298). Obviously, improvements were retained by Williamson on the unsold acreage.

Abbot's newly purchased property was east of Washington, sharing a border with the town common. As a physician, this location would have been an inappropriate one for an office. Willingham (1969:154-5) shows Abbot's office in the business district in 1820.

The dates from ceramic analysis cluster around a time in Abbot's life when his status was changing rapidly. In 1799, he was elected a state representative, and re-elected in 1802, 1803, 1808, and 1811. Abbot married in 1800, which was followed by the birth of three daughters, in 1807, 1809, and 1812. He was elected to Congress in 1817, serving until 1825. In 1812, Abbot was named a trustee of the University of Georgia. To the first convention of the National Pharmacopoeia, he was elected a delegate in 1820 (the preceding facts are from Thomas 1974). In addition to changes in Abbot's life,

Washington was a community growing in size and changing in composition.

Some changes to Washington which affected Abbot and his twelve acres are documented while others may only be inferred. In five transactions for the Toombs House property, including Abbot's purchase of 1797, the northern boundary is described in deeds by the name of the contiguous property owner (see Thomas 1974:54-66). Not until two years after Abbot's purchase is this boundary described otherwise. A deed of sale in 1799 of the property joining Abbot's on the north described the southern boundary as "Augusta R" (Wilkes County, Georgia, Deeds, Book RR:295). In a subsequent transaction that same year for the property, "Augusta R" is defined as "the Main Road leading from Washington to Augusta" (Wilkes County, Georgia, Deeds, Book XX:408). Abbot's northern boundary changed in form and consequently status. If a road comprised Abbot's northern boundary at the time of purchase in 1797, it must have been insignificant; that is, the road was private. As a minor feature of the landscape, the road was unmentioned in the deed description (Wilkes County, Georgia, Deeds, Book QQ:243). By 1799, a significant change had occurred along this boundary, for it was described as being the principal road leaving Washington for Augusta. A deed, dated 1 September 1787, described a boundary as the "Old Road." It was north of Abbot's property and may well have been the original road into the east side of Washington (Wilkes County, Georgia, Deeds, Book CC:167), which was subsequently replaced by "Augusta R."

Migration to the Georgia piedmont burgeoned after the Revolutionary War ended. Communities, such as Washington, in or near new Indian cessions, grew rapidly. Washington was legislated in 1783 as a town of 100 acres. By 1793, the legislature ordered the sale of property referred to as common of the town (Marbury and Crawford 1802:141-2). Washington was incorporated in 1805 by the legislature (General Assembly of the State of Georgia 1805). In 1813, the limits of the town were extended one-half mile (Lamar 1821:987) beyond the 1783 limits. This extension put Abbot's property in Washington. The town council, in 1821, authorized an extension of limits one mile on all sides (General Assembly of the State of Georgia 1821). Other transactions involving land around Abbot's property are interesting in the context of extending town limits.

In 1806, a year after the incorporation of the town, four and one-half acres bounding Abbot's property on the north along the "Main Road leading from Washington to Augusta" were sold (Wilkes County, Georgia, Deeds, Book XX:227). This property was subdivided for sale as individual tracts in 1813, the year an extension of town limits included it. In 1825, Abbot sold land on the northwest corner of his property fronting Augusta Road to a church.

As stated earlier, no substantive evidence of relocation of the Abbot portion of the Toombs House was found. Dates, however, from ceramic analysis clustered between 1804 and 1811. An examination of historical sources was undertaken in an attempt to ferret out circumstances which might support the hypothesis of relocation. A number were found.

From 1799, Abbot's status changed with an increase in familial, professional, and social responsibilities. Between 1797 and 1799, the northern boundary of Abbot's property changed in deed descriptions from the name of the bounded property owner to "Main Road leading from Washington to Augusta." From the originally legislated 100 acres of Washington of 1783, the town's limits expanded one-half mile in 1813, then to one mile in 1821. Property bounding Abbot's on the north side across Augusta Road, which was bought in 1806, was subdivided for sale in 1813. Abbot, in 1825, sold a portion of his property on the west side fronting Augusta Road.

From these circumstances, all of which suggest change, two inferences may be drawn regarding Abbot's house. It was expanded and relocated. A commensurate

increase in the size of Abbot's residence surely accompanied his ascendancy in
familial, professional, and social spheres. The northern boundary of his property changed in form, consequently in significance, from that of a line defined
by property owners' names to a major corridor of transportation east from Washington. Such a change could be a contributing factor in reorienting a house,
perhaps, relocating as well. The Toombs House property changed from rural status in 1797 to suburban, then to urban by 1813. Urban status, main-road fron-
tage, and adjacent property subdivided for sale, gave Abbot the beginnings of a
neighborhood. Finally, in 1825, Abbot sold a portion of his property on the
west side, fronting the Augusta Road. These circumstances of change considered
conjunctively with architectural and archaeological findings present a strong
argument for inferences of expansion and relocation. These inferences warrant
further investigation which is beyond the scope of this research.

Test Implication 5:   Dates derived from analysis of artifacts recovered from
                      features identified as consequences of house-moving acti-
                      vities will cluster around 1797.

     Archaeology in the basement of the Toombs House encountered no features or
other sources of information which could be identified as direct consequences
of relocating the Abbot house. No artifacts, therefore, were recovered for analysis.

Problem 5

     The fifth problem does not pertain directly to the interpretive and miti-
gative problems of the Toombs House. It was generated by preparatory research
for archaeology, during which this investigator thought some study on a more
general level of archaeology was warranted. The problem is that of determining

the season in which foundations were constructed by examining configuration and placement of footing trenches.

This problem is based on the assumption that occasionally footing trenches may be dug in a configuration different from one necessary to accommodate only a footing (see U.S. Department of the Navy 1972:53). If soil conditions, ground contour, or building specifications require a footing trench dug to a depth of more than a few inches, configuration and placement of the trench may vary. A brick mason must have access to the bottom of the trench in order to lay the first course of a footing. A configuration of the trench, namely width, might be expanded to accommodate the mason and the footing. If no cellar is included, the placement of the expanded trench width is optional and dependent on the mason. This option affords the mason a means of improving his working conditions by placing the expansion of the trench on the interior or exterior of the foundation he is to build. Given that footings and foundations are seldom, if ever, constructed with the benefit of shelter, the mason's decision on placement may be a consequence of the season in which his work begins or is about to enter.

If the expansion of a footing trench is placed on the interior of a foundation, one might assume construction began in the season of fall or winter, avoiding cold winds and dropping temperatures. If placement is on the exterior, then perhaps spring or summer was opted for in order to catch the warming sunshine or cooling breezes. These assumptions are tenuous and are tendered on little substantive data. Nonetheless, with footing trenches and their contents being investigated for other purposes, the hypothesis was tested at no additional cost in data recovery efforts. The hypothesis generated is as follows.

Hypothesis: The configurations and placement of a footing trench relative to the footing contained may indicate the season the foundation was constructed.

Two test implications were derived from this hypothesis. They are stated and discussed next.

Test Implication 1:   Footing trenches will be present for the foundations of the Toombs House.

This implication may seem obvious, but the kind and conditions of the archaeological resources of the Toombs House were unknown. Based on observations of the basement prior to archaeology and the fact that no archaeology was reported for the house, a condition of good was assumed as was the presence of footing trenches. Archaeology demonstrated that footing trenches existed for all foundations investigated (see Figure 35).

Test Implication 2:   Footing trenches with the form of expanded width relative to the interior or exterior face of contained footings will be found.

Abbot's deed, which is dated 16 December 1797, includes evidence that he was already constructing something on his property in this early winter month: ". . . said Doctor Joel Abbot is now a building" (Thomas 1974:100). Assuming this building was his house, the season of constructing the footings for Room A-4/5/6 (the Abbot portion) would probably be fall. If construction had just begun, the season could be early winter. Disregarding the problem of relocation of the house, an expectation for Room A-4/5/6 was formed. For the season of fall, or early winter, one would expect to find the placement of additional footing trench width on the interior of the foundations. This placement would shelter the mason from inclement conditions of the season. Regrettably, no other expectations were formed as no documentation of the construction of other portions of the house was recovered by preceding research.

In Room A-4/5/6, excavation revealed footing trenches which were of greater width than needed to accommodate footings (see Figure 35). The six foundation piers had footing trenches with a configuration of expanded width placed on their exterior. Contradiction appears when examining the trench around the fireplace, as additional trench width occurs on the interior in this area. This apparent contradiction is explained by the fact that construction of footings for a fireplace necessitates access from the interior due to shape. A mason simply could not complete, from an exterior position, the footings for a fireplace. Regardless of the season of fireplace construction, a mason requires access from the hearth side, that is, interior of the space to be served by the fireplace.

For Room A-1/2, additional trench width occurs on both the exterior and interior of the south wall (see Figure 35). Additional trench width occurs on the interior of the north wall, but this is not contradictory with the south wall. Two factors must be recalled. One, a feature, the dry well, occurs north of Room A-1/2 and pre-dates it. Two, the top of undisturbed subsoil around the dry well is almost a foot higher than the highest elevation of subsoil in A-1/2, suggesting building-site preparation. Access to the footing trench from the interior may have been the only option, as suggested by the occurrence of an older feature on the exterior of the north wall and the difference in elevation of subsoils. No excavation was conducted on the exterior of the north wall, so no data are available about any footing trenches which may have occurred there.

The placement of additional width of footing trenches of Room A-9/10 seems inconclusive (see Figure 35). The south wall of A-10 has a wide trench on the interior, but this was expected. If Room A-4/5/6 pre-dates A-9/10, then for

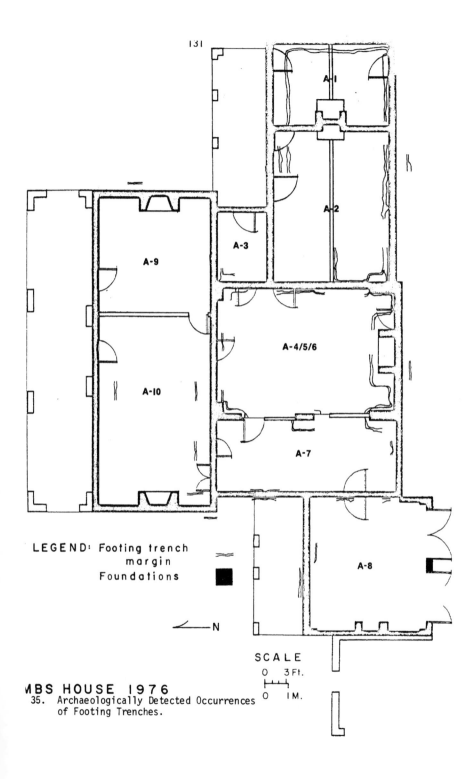

131

A-1

A-2

A-3

A-9

A-4/5/6

A-10

A-7

LEGEND: Footing trench
margin
Foundations

A-8

N

SCALE
0   3 Ft.
0   1 M.

ИBS HOUSE 1976
35.   Archaeologically Detected Occurrences
of Footing Trenches.

portions of foundations, juxtaposed construction of footings had to be done from the interior of A-9/10. Additional interior trench width of about the same dimension as that of the south wall occurs on the north wall. No excavation was conducted on the exterior of this wall. The west wall of A-9/10, however, has additional trench width on both sides. On the east wall, only an exterior exposure of the wall was possible due to preservation problems in Room A-9. A footing trench with additional width was found.

In Room A-7, a footing trench much narrower than those found in other rooms was revealed along both sides of the west wall (see Figure 35). The trench is slightly wider on the exterior. As this wall has no stepped footings, additional width for access may have been unnecessary. On the south wall of A-7, however, a footing trench of additional width on the interior was exposed (see Figure 35). An exterior exposure of this wall was unobtainable due to problems of disturbance of the ground.

For Room A-8, the only footing trench data come from the north wall. Additional trench width was placed on the interior of the wall (see Figure 35).

Unexpected Findings

Archaeology in the basement of the Toombs House revealed some resources for which no expectations had been formed. They will be described and discussed.

Room A-4/5/6

Discovered in the northwest corner of Room A-4/5/6 were two courses of brick laid as stretchers in a two-inch bond (see Ray 1961:123; Stoddard 1946: 24; see Figures 36-38). Excavation strategy was altered to determine the extent of this feature, as well as function and origin. The feature extended

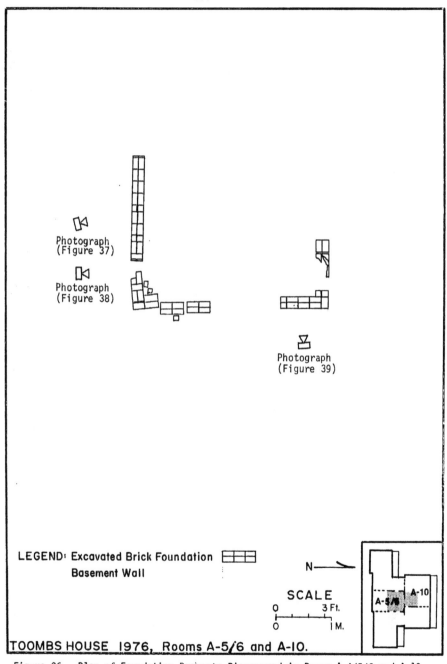

Figure 36.   Plan of Foundation Remnants Discovered in Rooms A-4/5/6 and A-10.

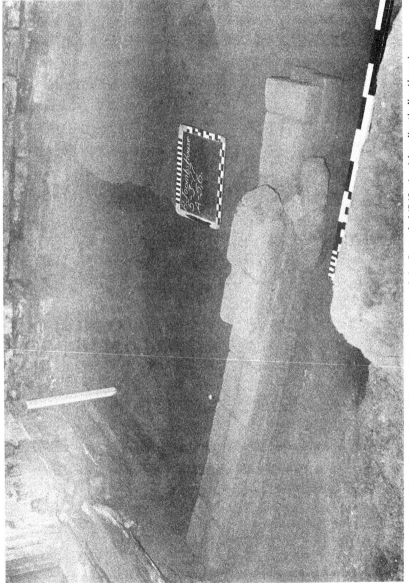

Figure 37. Remnants of Foundation Discovered in Room A-4/5/6, Looking North Northwest.

Figure 38. Remnants of Foundation Discovered in Room A-4/5/6, Looking North.

eastward for about ten feet, then turned northward at a right angle. The brick stopped just inside the south wall of Room A-10, where they were interrupted by a footing trench. A portion of a footing trench was found on the north side of the feature along its east-west segment. This trench and the pattern in which the brick were laid indicated the feature was a remnant foundation. Unfortunately, no diagnostic artifacts were recovered which could be clearly associated with the foundation. Construction of A-4/5/6 and subsequent use of the area had severely disturbed the ground around this remnant foundation.

Extensions of this foundation were sought in Rooms A-7 and A-10. A unit (E10.6 N27.6) had been excavated in Room A-7 just west of the unit of A-4/5/6, in which the feature was found (E5.1 N26.9). No evidence of the feature had been encountered. A cursory search for additional remnants in A-10 was made, but nothing was found. The inadequacy of this effort was demonstrated when an additional find was made after field work had concluded (see Figures 36 and 39). As the footing trench on the south side of the wall of A-10 had interrupted this remnant foundation, so did the footing trench on the north side of this wall. Subsequently, the floor of A-10 was probed with a quarter-inch-diameter metal rod for other remnants. None were detected.

Few data beyond the presence, composition, and form of this foundation are available. Brick size (2-1/2" height x 4" width x 8-1/4" length) was smaller than those used in the piers of Room A-4/5/6, but similar to those of other rooms (see Figure 24). No used brick were observed, that is, ones with whitewashed, glazed, or similarly altered surfaces. In the second course of the east-west segment in A-4/5/6, two headers occur just west of the corner where the foundation turns northward. Their presence and spacing are interesting, but unexplained. Based on a wall width of eight inches, the assumption is made that this foundation supported one story (Dalzell and Townsend 1954:47; Graham

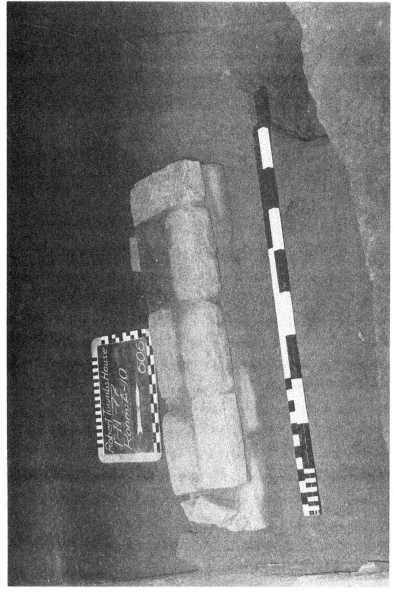

Figure 39. Remnants of Foundation Discovered in Room A-10, Looking West.

1924:305; Kidder and Parker 1956:235, Table 1; Stoddard 1946:62; U.S. Department of the Navy 1972:182), no more than two. Finally, the dimension of overall width of the area demarked by the foundation, twelve and one-half feet, was imposed on other spaces of the house and outbuildings, but no match was made. The presence of this foundation is a significant factor. The Toombs House is obviously not the first historic structure to occupy this site.

Room A-10

As excavation was conducted in Room A-10, a pattern was recognized in profiles of some of the units. Just beneath the sand base of a brick floor was a series of undulations of the surface of the clay subsoil. In the north and south profiles, on about thirty-inch centers, were what appeared to be trenches (see Figure 40, profiles A-A[1] and B-B[1]). In the western portion of the room, some of the "trenches" were excavated. Based on observations of this sample, the extent of these features was extrapolated to the entirety of A-10 (see Figure 40). From a small test unit in the doorway between A-9 and A-10, the features may be extrapolated to Room A-9 (see Figure 40, profile A-A[1]).

Preceding research had recovered no evidence of this kind of feature occurring in Room A-9/10. Based on symmetry of placement of the trenches, some form of support for a floor is indicated. Obviously, at the time of construction, the proximity of framing, assumed to be wood, to the ground was not considered; with plenty of wood available, perhaps it was not a factor. These trenches add data of the original surface treatment of the space to our knowledge of Room A-9/10.

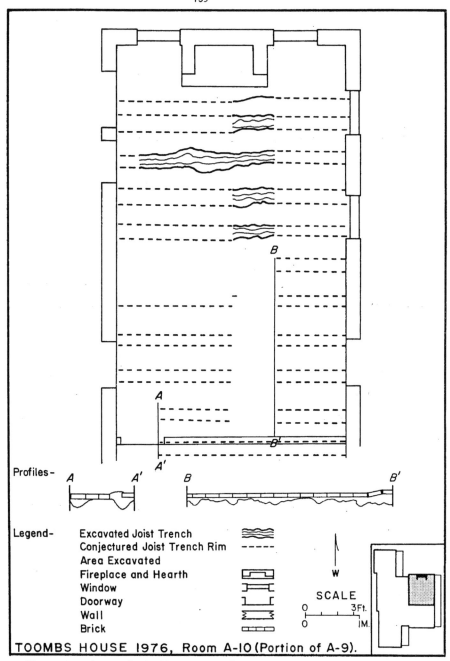

Profiles—

Legend—
Excavated Joist Trench
Conjectured Joist Trench Rim
Area Excavated
Fireplace and Hearth
Window
Doorway
Wall
Brick

SCALE
0   3Ft.
0   1M.

W

TOOMBS HOUSE 1976, Room A-10 (Portion of A-9).

Figure 40.   Archaeologically Detected "Joist" Trenches with Extrapolations.

CHAPTER 6

GENERAL RESULTS

The results of analysis for each of the problems addressed by this research will be discussed in general. The order of treatment is that which has
been maintained throughout this report.

Results for Problems Addressed

Problem 1

For the first problem, which concerns the number of phases in which the
Toombs House was constructed, the results of archaeological research corroborated the findings of preceding research. Architectural and historical investigations (Neal 1976; Thomas 1974) each identified four phases of construction
(see Figure 17), which were temporally distinct. Archaeological research strategy incorporated these findings by assuming these identified phases of construction. The recovery of evidence to support this assumption was focused on
the foundations of the house.

From foundations, evidence regarding footing trench configurations, building materials, building practices, structural distinction, and dates of construction was retrieved. A collective analysis of the evidence resulted in the
identification of four phases of construction: A-1/2, A-4/5/6, A-9/10, and A-8.
No sequence of construction is implied in this presentation. Room A-3, of
course, is not included, as three of its four walls are the exteriors of other
rooms (see Figure 17). Room A-7 is another problem.

In Room A-7, only two of the walls belong to this area, as the north and east walls are exteriors of A-10 and A-4/5/6, respectively. The south and west walls of A-7 are comprised almost entirely of modern brick above ground, obviously replacing deteriorated brick. Excavation revealed a continuous foundation of brick beneath the surface of the ground. As this room is beneath the front porch of the Abbot portion (Neal 1976) of the house, the form of its enclosure is uncertain. With Room A-4/5/6 comprised of piers, the continuous brick enclosure of the space beneath a porch is incongruous. Neal's (1976) elevation drawing depicts a porch supported by piers. Regrettably, no evidence to support or refute Neal was recovered from A-7. The inconclusiveness of the investigation of this area, however, is not a problem for deriving results. The dates from ceramic analysis may reflect the altered status of this space after relocation occurred. This space was enclosed to conform with the rest of the basement.

Problem 2

For the identified phases of construction, the second problem was that of establishing a temporal sequence for them. Based on architectural and historical research, a sequence was hypothesized: first, A-4/5/6/7; second, A-9/10; third, A-1/2; and fourth, A-8. Foundations again were investigated, but not for evidence of spatial composition. The temporal order of phases was the subject of investigation. Configuration of footing trenches, building materials, building practices, and artifactual contents of associated features were investigated for evidence as to the sequence in which the phases of the house were constructed.

Evidence regarding configuration of footing trenches as well as building materials and practices was informative in developing a temporal sequence for construction of phases. Footing trenches of A-4/5/6 were shown to have been affected in such a way by construction activities of A-1/2 and A-9/10 to indicate A-4/5/6 was older than either A-1/2 or A-9/10. Unfortunately, phases A-1/2, A-9/10, and A-8 are structurally discontiguous, so no opportunity was available to investigate the direct effects of construction of any one of these on another. Building materials and practices were insufficiently distinctive to provide temporal order.

Analysis of artifacts recovered from footing trenches and associated features was informative, but not in the way which was anticipated. Dates resulting from ceramic analysis clustered tightly regardless of whether the contents of entire ceramic assemblages (phases of construction) or of undisturbed contexts of those phases (footing trenches) were considered (see Tables 6 and 7). For the former, the spread is less than four and one-half years (4.2); for the latter, less than two years (1.7). Results of analysis of the ceramic assemblage of identified phases give this sequence: first, A-9/10 (1806.5); second, A-8 (1807.6); third, A-1/2 (1809.0); fourth, A-4/5/6/7 (1809.3). For the analisis of ceramics from undisturbed construction features, the sequence is: first, A-8 (1806.7); second, A-9/10 (1807.7); third, A-4/5/6/7 (1808.0); fourth, A-1/2 (1808.4). Sequences are derived, but their reliability is dubious because of the proximity of dates from either source of data and the conflict with the results of other forms of research (see Table 6).

Problem 3

Based on architectural and historical research, an appendage may have been removed from the east side of Room A-4/5/6 prior to the construction of Room A-1/2. The problem was to recover evidence which would provide additional information about any appendage. Archaeology conducted in Room A-1/2 encountered no evidence of any former appendage. This absence of evidence, however, is inconclusive. The highest elevation of subsoil in Room A-1/2 is about one foot below the top of subsoil around the dry well just north of A-1/2 in Room A-3. Prior to the construction of A-1/2, the site may have been altered in preparation. During this activity, evidence of any former appendages may have been graded away.

Problem 4

Thomas (1974), in his historical research, cited a source which indicates the Abbot portion (A-4/5/6) of the Toombs House was moved back from the road, supposedly East Robert Toombs Avenue. When this move happened is unspecified, but the implication was during Abbot's residency (1797-1825). With only secondary information available, what one might expect to find was uncertain. Preparatory research for archaeology, therefore, sought information about house-moving practices and procedures. This effort was not successful, but it was informative in general.

Assuming the house was not disassembled entirely, or even partially, evidence of events and circumstances of moving was sought. No archaeological evidence of this type was recovered. The site, however, served a previous structure. In Rooms A-4/5/6 and A-10, remnants of a foundation were discovered. Circumstantial evidence indicates that the acreage Abbot bought in 1797 was unimproved -- five dollars per acre. Also, the early 1800's was a period of growth and change in Washington and Wilkes County, some of which may have led Abbot to move his house. The original site of the house before the hypothesized relocation is unknown. For the Abbot portion of the Toombs House, circumstantial evidence suggests relocation, but no substantive data were archaeologically recovered which directly support the occurrence of such an event.

Problem 5

By examining the configuration and placement of footing trenches, something about the season in which foundations were constructed was hoped to be learned. The only documentation of the season of any construction was Abbot's deed to twelve acres. On 16 December 1797, the date of the deed, Abbot was "now a building." Assumed was the fact that placement of additional footing-trench width on the interior or exterior of foundations reflected a mason's decision. This decision may have been based on the climatic conditions, with the mason anticipating shielding effects of rising foundations.

For Room A-4/5/6, a season of fall or winter was expected, given the date on the deed. Footing trenches with additional width were found for all piers. This width occurred on the exterior of the piers. Inferred from this placement was a season of warmth, perhaps spring or summer. Either some variable other than season affected placement of additional footing-trench width, or these trenches were not the result of "building" mentioned in Abbot's 1797 deed.

The footing trench for the foundation walls of Room A-9/10 had additional width on the exterior and interior. However, the latter was about twice the width of the former. Based on the assumption of seasonal placement, the foundations of Room A-9/10 were begun in the fall or winter.

Room A-1/2 is more complex than either of the preceding rooms. As previously mentioned, elevation of subsoil drops almost a foot from just north of A-1/2 at the dry well to inside the room itself. Placement of a footing trench of additional width on the interior of the north wall may have been the only option.

For Room A-8, additional footing-trench width was found on the interior of the north wall. This placement suggests foundations were begun in the fall or winter.

Comparison of Results

In this section, the results of archaeological research are compared with those of preceding architectural and historical research. For the first problem of number of phases of construction, the results of archaeological research corresponded with those of architectural and historical efforts. This preceding research resulted in the identification of four phases of construction. They were A-1/2, A-4/5/6/7, A-9/10, and A-8. Framing of the house provided the basis of information for architectural analysis (Neal 1976). Most of the historical evidence for phasing came from secondary sources (see Thomas 1974:101, 103). By examining foundations and associated features, archaeology identified four phases of construction which concurred with the results of preceding research. The phases are A-1/2, A-4/5/6/7, A-9/10, and A-8.

Opposition exists between results of historical and architectural research and that of archaeology regarding the problem of sequence of identified phases. Preceding research proposed this sequence: A-4/5/6/7 (1797), A-9/10 (c. 1830's), A-1/2 (c. 1870's), and A-8 (c. 1870's). The result of archaeological research was a narrow temporal sequence: A-4/5/6/7 (1806), A-9/10 (1808), A-8 (1808), and A-1/2 (1809).

Secondary sources comprise most of the documentation for the dates derived through historical research (see Thomas 1974:101, 103). The reliability and accuracy of these dates are uncertain. A single primary source, Abbot's deed, stated that, in 1797, "the said Doctor Abbot is now a building" (Thomas 1974: 57). We know neither what he was building, nor where on the twelve acres he had just purchased. Architectural research analyzed the frame of the house, deriving dates from framing styles, techniques, etc.

Archaeology began with the dates derived by preceding research for phases of construction. It focused on foundations and associated features of the basement. Using South's Mean Ceramic Dating Formula (MCOF), ceramics excavated from the basement were analyzed. Dates obtained from both undisturbed resources clustered narrowly in the first decade of the nineteenth century (see Table 4). Ceramic assemblages of three rooms were small ($<$ 100 fragments each), while for two rooms, assemblages were large ($>$ 1,000 fragments each). The remaining rooms ranged between these (see Table 4).

A cumulative consideration of historical data of the Washington-Wilkes area reveals the early 1800's as a period of change and development. The same may be said for Joel Abbot (see Thomas 1974). The rapid growth of the Georgia piedmont and the ascendancy of Abbot in social, professional, and political spheres of Georgia correlate with the dates derived archaeologically. A man of Abbot's status in Washington surely resided in something larger than what today is referred to as the Abbot portion of the Toombs House.

The opposing dates of the sequence of construction are derived from different sources of data by different means of investigation. In the absence of primary documentation supporting any sequence, interpretation must depend on indirect, that is, secondary and circumstantial, sources of information. These sources provide contexts in which to evaluate all of the results of research.

The remaining two problems of appendage removal and relocation of the house were inconclusive. Evidence of appendage removal as supplied by architectural and historical research was unconfirmed by archaeology in Room A-1/2. No evidence of a former appendage, or its construction or removal was found. However, some evidence indicates the site of A-1/2 had been prepared for construction. Results of this activity may have been grading which removed archaeological evidence of former appendages.

Relocation of the house was not addressed by architectural and historical research in a major way. No evidence of relocation was recovered during architectural analysis (Neal 1976: 1981 personal communication). Historical evidence consisted of a single secondary source (Bowen 1950: 102). Archaeological research found no resources which could be identified as direct consequences of relocating the Abbot portion of the house. Other archaeological data, however, demonstrate that the site of the Toombs House, namely Rooms A-4/5/6, and A-10, had been the site of a previous structure. Dates derived from ceramic analysis indicate that the first decade of the eighteenth century was one of intense construction activity at the Abbot house.

The fifth problem concerning footing trenches and season of construction will not be treated here. No other reported research was found with which to make comparisons.

CHAPTER 7

GENERAL CONCLUSIONS

To begin this section, a restatement of problems and hypotheses is needed before considering conclusions. Of the five problems addressed, four were generated by preceding architectural and historical research for the Toombs House. The fifth one resulted from preparatory research for archaeology at the Toombs House. The problems are outlined and then discussed.

The Problems Addressed

1. Number of phases in which the house was built;

2. Temporal sequence of identified phases of construction;

3. Removal of appendages from the Abbot portion of the house;

4. Relocation of the Abbot portion of the house; and

5. Season, or seasons, in which foundations were constructed.

These problems directed archaeological strategy and tactics. During the review of proposed restoration plans and specifications, the need for archaeology was formally recognized and addressed. Certain prescribed restoration measures would disturb or destroy archaeological resources in the basement. These resources were acknowledged as having a potential for solving some interpretive problems identified by preceding research. Additional preparatory research for archaeology generated a problem which could be investigated during archaeological research addressing the interpretive problems.

For each problem, a working hypothesis was generated. Each is presented in the order which reflects the outline of problems.

- 148 -

1. The Toombs House was constructed in at least four temporally distinct phases.

2. The temporal sequence of the phases of construction is: first, Room A-4/5/6/7; second, Room A-9/10; third, Room A-1/2; and fourth, Room A-8.

3. Prior to the construction of Room A-1/2, an appendage was attached to the east side of Room A-4/5/6.

4. The Abbot portion of the house, Room A-4/5/6/7, was moved back, that is, south, from East Robert Toombs Avenue.

5. The configuration and placement of a footing trench relative to the footing contained may indicate the season in which a foundation was constructed.

With this restatement of problems and their hypotheses, specific conclusions will be tendered. Conclusions relative to each hypothesis in the order the hypotheses were presented will be stated and discussed.

Conclusions Relative to Hypotheses

For the first hypothesis of four temporally distinct phases of construction, five test implications were derived (see "Working Hypotheses" in Introduction). The implications focused on foundations, footings, footing trenches, artifacts, and associated features. An examination of the configurations of footing trenches, of building materials, of building practices, of structural continuity, and of artifacts led to these conclusions.

1. The Toombs House was built in four phases, as identified by architectural and historical research and as hypothesized in archaeological research: Room A-1/2, Room A-4/5/6, Room A-9/10, and Room A-8 (no temporal sequence is implied).

2. The four identified phases of construction are distinguishable on the basis of structure and configurations of features with Room A-4/5/6 superceded by Room A-1/2 and Room A-9/10; Room A-9/10 precedes Room A-1/2; and Room A-8 is structurally discontinuous from the aforementioned and cannot be treated.

3. Ceramic analysis produced dates for each of the identified phases of construction, but they are so close to each other in time as to provide no reliable sequence: A-1/2 (1808.4, 1809.0), A-4/5/6/7 (1808.0, 1809.3), A-9/10 (1807.7, 1806.5), A-8 (1806.9, 1807.6) (see Table 5).

We conclude for the first hypothesis that the Toombs House was constructed in four phases, which are A-1/2, A-4/5/6, A-8, and A-9/10. As for temporal distinction of the phases, A-4/5/6 is the oldest. It is followed by A-9/10, then A-1/2, based on structural data. The placement of A-8 in this sequence is uncertain for two reasons. First, Room A-8 is structurally discontinuous from the other foundations, so no sequence based on configurations of foundation features was ascertainable. Second, as the results of ceramic analysis were not temporally distinctive for any of the phases, no assistance was provided by this means.

The second hypothesis contained a temporal sequence for the identified phases of construction, beginning with the oldest: A-4/5/6/7, A-9/10, A-1/2, and A-8. Four test implications were derived. Again, configurations of footing trenches, building materials, building practices, and artifacts comprised the sources of data. As for the first hypothesis, footing-trench configurations were limited by structural discontinuity. Building materials and building practices were found to be suggestive of temporal order in only a relative manner, lacking any dominant horizon markers. Dates derived from ceramic analysis were uninformative for establishing a temporal sequence for identified phases of construction.

The only sequence which may be established is a relative one based on a cumulative consideration of structural attributes of the house. Features resulting from the construction of A-4/5/6 were found to be directly affected, that is, modified, by construction features of A-1/2 and A-9/10. The occurrence of intensive site preparation in A-1/2 indicates that A-9/10 precedes A-1/2 in time. As for A-8, its place in this sequence of construction is uncertain due to its lack of structural contiguity. For the hypothesized temporal sequence of phases the following conclusion is drawn:

Room A-4/5/6 was constructed first, followed by Room 9/10, then Room A-1/2. The placement of A-8 in this sequence is uncertain.

The third hypothesis dealt with the removal of an appendage from the east side of Room A-4/5/6. Three test implications were investigated concerning remnants of structure, remnants of construction, and diagnostic artifacts. Excavation encountered no remnants of structure or construction, nor recovered any artifacts other than those associated with the period represented by Room A-1/2. The following conclusion was drawn:

Based on topographic data, differences of the elevation of subsoil in A-1/2 and A-3, the area of A-1/2 had been prepared for construction by removing about a foot of soil. All archaeological evidence of any previous function of the area was a victim of this site preparation, including any appendage.

The fourth hypothesis resulted from a suggestion in a secondary source (Bowen 1950), that the Abbot portion of the house was moved back from the road. Vagueness plagued this situation. The form of such a move, intact, partially disassembled, or completely disassembled, was unknown. The original site was unknown. The direction of the move, south, was based on the assumption that the "road" mentioned by Bowen was East Robert Toombs Avenue. Compounding vagueness was the fact that archaeology was restricted to the basement of the Toombs House. For the hypothesis of relocation, five test implications were derived. No evidence of activities directly attributable to moving the Abbot portion was identified, or consequences of moving activities encountered. Evidence of previous use of the site was found.

The fifth hypothesis, which was generated by preparatory research for archaeology, stated that the season of construction might be inferred from the configuration and placement of footing trenches relative to footings. Two test implications were derived. Undisturbed footing trenches were found in all excavated exposures of foundations. For the various phases of construction previously identified, footing trenches of greater width than needed to accommodate footings were exposed. The placement of this additional width for some phases exhibited a pattern. For Room A-4/5/6, additional width occurred on the exterior of the foundation piers. Additional width occurred on both sides of the foundation walls of A-9/10, but greater width was found on the interior of the room. In Room A-1/2, a pattern is difficult to discern on first view. A trench with additional width exists on the interior of the north wall, while additional width on the south wall occurs on the exterior. No exposure of the exterior of the north wall was excavated, but based on topographic data, the occurrence of a wide trench is unlikely. The subsoil on the exterior of the north wall is at a higher elevation than on the interior, which suggests more effort would be required to lay brick from the exterior. Besides, the interior of A-1/2 was prepared for construction by lowering the ground level.

For the south wall of A-1/2, additional footing-trench width occurs on the interior of the south and east walls. The assumption is made that the additional width on the exterior of the south wall also occurs on the east one.

The pattern of placement of additional trench width for A-1/2 is on the exterior; the north wall appears to offer no option for placement.

In Room A-8, exposures of the foundation of the north wall on both sides show that additional footing-trench width is placed on the interior.

For Room A-7, almost no additional trench width occurs along the west wall, although the side of the trench slopes away from the foundation on the exterior more than on the interior. However, the south wall has a footing trench with additional width on the interior. This additional width may have been required as the bottom of the footing trench has an elevation of about 22.7 feet above arbitrary datum (see Figure 16). The bottom of the footing trench on the north end of the west wall is 23.5 feet above arbitrary datum, indicating a reduction in the number of courses of brick. This reduction was verified archaeologically, when the bottom of the trench rose one course of brick from an elevation of 22.76 feet (about the same elevation as the bottom of the footing trench on the south wall, 22.7 feet) to 22.9 feet above arbitrary datum.

The eight-inch-wide walls of A-7 have no footings. The bottom course of brick is a double row of stretchers on the south wall and a portion of the west wall. At the point where the number of courses of brick changes, the west wall's bottom course becomes headers. The gradient of the subsoil declines north to south in the room from 24.3 to 23.4 feet above arbitrary datum. This difference of about one foot corresponds to that of elevation differences of footing-trench bottoms, on the north end of the west wall 23.5 feet and on the south wall 22.7 feet above arbitrary datum. For A-7, the significance of additional trench width on the interior of the south wall may be that placement is a product of gradient rather than a mason's attempt to enhance his working environment.

Based on the analysis of data derived from the configurations and

placement of footing trenches, the following conclusions are drawn. Construction of the foundations of Room A-4/5/6 was begun in the spring or summer. The
foundations of Room A-9/10 were begun in the fall or winter. Room A-1/2 was
begun in the spring or summer. Fall or winter was the season in which Room A-8
had its foundations started. Finally, Room A-7 appears to have begun in the
fall or winter, but the gradient change makes this inference dubious. The conclusions are obviously tenuous and must be corroborated with evidence from
other sources.

Discussion of Unanticipated Findings

During the archaeological segment of Toombs House research, a number of
features were encountered which were unanticipated. Neither architectural and
historical research, nor preparatory research for archaeology, had come across
anything hinting of these occurrences. Some add to our understanding of the
structure, while others compound its complexity. Each will be discussed in the
context of general conclusions of this research.

The most significant of the unanticipated finds were the remnants of a
foundation occurring in Rooms A-4/5/6 and A-10 (see Figure 36). Based on
Abbot's deed to twelve acres on which he was building, the assumption could be
made that this was the original site of the house. A secondary source (Bowen
1950), however, relates that the Abbot portion was moved back from the road.
For the Toombs House, the presence of the foundation in the basement is ex-
tremely important to interpretation.

The function and the origin of the foundation are unknown. The dimensions
and location of it are now recorded. For the Toombs House, two alternatives
occur. One, when Abbot built his house in 1797, he had to remove a structure
from the site for his new home. The problem with this is that Abbot purchased

the land at five dollars per acre. This does not sound like improved property. Of course, the foundations could have been in ruins when Abbot bought the property, but we have no records of any prior historic activity on the twelve acres. Two, a building had to be torn down so that the Abbot portion of the house could be relocated to this site. Certainly, Abbot had constructed outbuildings around his first house. With relocation, however, an outbuilding had to be removed so that the newly chosen site could be used.

Of these alternatives, the evidence supports the latter. Abbot purchased twelve unimproved acres for sixty dollars on which he was building. We do not know what he was building, but inferring a house is not unreasonable. As a new resident of Washington, practicing medicine, a home on the edge of town and an office in the business district is an expected distribution of activities. In addition to settlement patterning, other evidence supports relocation.

Analysis of archaeologically recovered artifacts resulted in a series of dates clustering in the first decade of the 1800's (see Table 8). These dates correlate well with Abbot's ascendancy in familial, social, and political spheres of Washington and the state. He was elected a state representative in 1799, and again in the following years of 1802, 1803, 1808, and 1811. Abbot married in 1800, and in 1807, his first child was born; two more followed, the second in 1809 and the last in 1812. In 1817, he was elected a representative to Congress, where he served until 1825. In 1812, Abbot was named a trustee of the University of Georgia, and in 1820, he was elected a delegate to the first convention of the National Pharmacopoeia. Attendant to Abbot's political, social, and biological prosperity would have been a commensurate change in his residence, expanding to accommodate additional residents, as well as the statuses of politician, husband, parent, trustee, delegate, etc. (see Thomas 1974: 4-11). The Toombs House underwent extensive alteration during Abbot's residency. One of the alterations may have been relocation as indicated by the occurrence of a remnant foundation in the basement. Even though relocation was hypothesized, evidence for house-moving was insufficient. The remnant foundation certainly indicates the present site had served another structure before the construction of the oldest portion of the Toombs House, raising the probability for the occurrence of relocation.

Somewhat less significant to the interpretation of the house was the discovery of evidence of a framed floor in Rooms A-9/10. Beneath the extant framed floor of A-9/10, which was removed as a restoration activity, was a brick floor. In Room A-10, the surface of the brick exhibited no wear, and the brick were assumed to have been a moisture barrier. In A-9, a brick floor exhibiting severe wear was exposed by the removal of a framed floor which rested on the brick. Because of the fragile condition of the brick in this room, none was removed. A small unit was excavated in the doorway between A-9 and A-10, in addition to numerous units in A-10 (see Figure 40).

In A-10, a series of parallel trenches on a thirty-inch center was discovered (see Figure 40). Based on the distribution and shape of these trenches, an inference was made. They had once contained the joists of a framed floor. This trenching probably reflects an attempt to obtain as much ceiling height as possible. From this indication of flooring, at least three inferences can be drawn for Room A-9/10. One, the room was enclosed from the time of construction of foundations. The difference between dates derived from ceramics recovered from these "joist" trenches and the footing trenches is less than three years in Room A-10 (see Table 6). Such a floor would have required protection from the weather. Two, the present interior of the room and its interpretation may have nothing to do with the original function of the space. We simply do not know what purpose this area may have served. Three, Room A-9/10 was added to Room A-4/5/6. If the rooms had been built simultaneously, or Room A-9/10 first, elevation of the ceiling would have been appropriately planned. This problem of adequate ceiling height may have been a reason for lowering the ground level in Room A-1/2, providing an eight-foot ceiling, instead of one slightly more than seven feet, as in A-9/10.

A finding which added to the complexity of the Toombs House was the presence of used brick scattered throughout the foundations of Rooms A-1/2, A-4/5/6, and A-9/10. The dominant indicator of previous use was the occurrence of whitewash on surfaces of brick. Other indicators were glazing, mortar remnants, and brick color and size. These used brick were observed in footings, piers, walls, and fireplaces. Significance of the presence of used brick in the foundations is evidence of relocation.

Another unanticipated finding dealt with bonding, that is, interlocking of brick. In two rooms, A-1/2 and A-4/5/6, foundations were exposed which were not bonded. The brick wall between A-1 and A-2 was not bonded with the walls which it abuts. A reason for this absence of bonding could not be determined. One may conjecture that it was added later. How much later, though, is confusing. Brick size and masonry style are similar to the walls it abuts. Perhaps the lack of bonding reflects a building practice found elsewhere in the house.

The piers on the south side of Room A-4/5/6 are not bonded to the fireplace which they abut. The unbonded wall in A-1/2 contains fireplaces which share a chimney. Given the additional size and weight of fireplaces, a problem of differential settlement with surrounding load-bearing foundations may have dictated this practice. Significance of this practice is unknown, and no conclusions for the Toombs House are drawn.

The last unanticipated finding was a product of analysis rather than observation. Using South's Mean Ceramic Dating Formula, ceramics from undisturbed

contexts such as footing trenches, hearth fill, joist trenches, and construction layers were analyzed. The results were dates clustering in the first
decade of the nineteenth century (see Table 6, average of MCDF dates). Even
analysis of the total ceramic assemblage of each room, as identified by preceding research, gave similar dates (see Table 4, total ceramic assemblage). All
of the dates disagree with results of architectural and historical research
(see Table 5). However, if the dates are considered in the contexts of other
evidence, some support for them is garnered.

With the dates of the four identified phases of construction clustering in
the early 1800's, two aspects of Toombs House interpretation are addressed, relocation and expansion of the house. A secondary historical source (Bowen
1950) mentions that the Abbot portion was moved back from the road. Other historical sources, deed records and legislation, provide circumstantial evidence
of reasons for relocation. Deeds of five transactions involving the Toombs
House property, including Abbot's purchase in 1797 (see Thomas 1974:54-66), define the northern boundary by naming the owner of the bounded property. Not
until a transaction in 1799 can one deduce that a property with a southern
boundary described as "Augusta R" constituted Abbot's northern boundary (Wilkes
County, Georgia, Deeds, Book RR:295). In a subsequent transaction for the same
property that year, "Augusta R" is defined as "the Main Road leading from Washington to Augusta" (Wilkes County, Georgia, Deeds, Book XX:408). Based on this
information, the assumption was made that if a road did comprise the northern
boundary of Abbot's property (Toombs House land), it was insignificant. Some-
time after Abbot's purchase in 1797, change occurred. By insignificant is
meant that any road along this boundary was not a public thoroughfare. Obviously, the road, if it existed at the time of Abbot's purchase, was not significant enough to be incorporated into the boundary description of Abbot's

property (Wilkes County, Georgia, Deeds, Book QQ:243), or those of contiguous properties to his north.

As the population of the piedmont grew and developing communities expanded, "urban sprawl" began. From the 100 acres legislated for Washington in 1783, the town soon expanded. In 1805, the state legislature incorporated Washington (General Assembly of the State of Georgia 1805). By 1813, the town limits were extended one-half mile (Lamar 1821:987) beyond the originally legislated boundary of 1783. The town council authorized extending town limits in 1821 one mile on all sides (General Assembly of the State of Georgia 1821). By 1825, the Toombs House property was in Washington, when Abbot sold land on the west side of his property to the Presbyterian church (Bowen 1950:160). The inference may be drawn that Abbot was not selling a portion of his front yard. His house probably faced north toward the main road from Washington to Augusta. In addition to these factors, Gilbert had bought four and one-half acres in 1806 on the north side of this "Main Road leading from Washington to Augusta" across from Abbot (Wilkes County, Georgia, Deeds, Book XX:227). By 1813, he had subdivided this property and was selling tracts of it; this action coincides with extension of town limits.

With construction of the Toombs House demonstrated to have occurred in four phases, all of which date according to ceramic analysis in the early 1800's, the proximity of dates may be partly a product of environmental change. The Toombs House property shifted from a rural to suburban, then to an urban setting during Abbot's ownership. Other archaeological evidence, such as remnants of a foundation in the basement and used brick in foundations of the house, indicate change. A consequence may have been relocation of some of the Toombs House, the Abbot portion.

In addition, the clustering of dates indicates the house was expanded in a short period of time, probably soon after relocation. An examination of Joel Abbot's life history exhibits a trend warranting an expanding residence. Though trained as a physician, Abbot was elected to state office, then national office. He married and became the father of three daughters. All these events define a need for space beyond the portion of the house referred to as Abbot's. Family size and community status dictated a larger residence. Abbot's ascendancy in political, familial, and social spheres of Washington correlates with dates derived from ceramic analysis. The early 1800's was a period of change for the residents of the Toombs House as well as the house itself -- relocation and expansion.

Contributions to Preceding Research

Archaeological research at the Toombs House contributed to the preceding architectural and historical research in these ways. First, archaeology resulted in observations which provided additional confirmation of preceding results. Architectural and historical research identified four phases of construction for the Toombs House. Exposures of the foundations by archaeology also observed the same four phases, substantiating preceding research results at a fundamental level in the occurrence of the house. Archaeology, also, resulted in exposing remnants of a foundation beneath the ground in Rooms A-4/5/6 and A-10. The Toombs House apparently was not the original historic use of the site. Observations of this remnant foundation garner support for the idea generated by historical research that the Abbot portion (A-4/5/6/7) of the house had been relocated, that is, moved back from the road.

Second, analysis of ceramics recovered archaeologically resulted in dates for the identified phases of house construction. The dates cluster so narrowly, though, as to define no temporal sequence of construction for the identified phases. In addition, the dates of the phases conflict with those derived by preceding research. However, historical research demonstrated a period of change in Washington and in Abbot's life which coincides with the dates obtained from ceramic analysis. From this period may be inferred change to the house, which was manifested in relocation and expansion.

Recommendations - General and Specific

General

The role of the interdisciplinary approach to the investigation of the Toombs House should be vigorously interpreted. An example would be to elaborate the identification of the phases in which the house was constructed. Investigating the same problem from more than single perspective broadened the scope of research. More sources of information were sought and tapped by a variety of means. The consequences are of benefit not only to the subject of investigation, but to all involved disciplines of inquiry. A solution or answer to the addressed problem or question receives interdisciplinary scrutiny. Methods and techniques which were employed by each discipline receive confirmation or refutation. They garner evidence regarding their effectiveness and utility in research. The overall benefits for a resource such as the Toombs House is that the interpretation and preservation values for which public acquisition was undertaken are maximized.

Regarding evidence of former appendages, archaeology encountered nothing in the area of Room A-1/2. This occurrence, however, should be used to illustrate the value of a multidisciplinary approach to a resource as complex as the Toombs House. Of course, this unfortunate result could happen to any form of investigation. Identified sources of information are simply absent. This may be a product of poorly formulated research, inefficient or ineffective methods and techniques of investigation, or something about the source being sought.

It may have never existed, may be in an unexpected form, or may have been des.-
troyed. With a multidisciplinary approach, the need of a solution to a particular problem may be addressed by another discipline. Results may become more
significant in the light of tapping additional sources of solutions, but, as in
this instance, the results also may become less significant. Multiple confirmation or refutation is a most desirable product of the multidisciplinary approach to investigation.

The problem of determining whether or not a portion of the Toombs House
was moved (relocated) is an excellent illustration of building a case on circumstantial evidence. The only source identifying this event of moving is a
secondary historical reference (Bowen 1950). Efforts of history, architecture,
and archaeology found no primary sources which could be identified as absolute
evidence of relocation. However, if evidence recovered by these various disciplines of investigation is examined collectively, an inference of relocation
may be drawn. Each form of investigation has identified a set of circumstances
regarding the house. None is informative about the problem if considered in
isolation from the other sets. Examined collectively, though, corresponding
circumstances may be identified. Then, if those circumstances are considered
as a set, even though they may not provide a substantive solution, they may
suggest trends, patterns, or similarities warranting further investigation.
Again, the multidisciplinary approach provides a means of tendering solutions
in the absence of substantive evidence.

Specific

1. For the temporal sequence of phases of construction, the discrepancy
   between dates derived archaeologically and those from preceding research should be ignored. Both sets of dates should be incorporated

into interpretation. The resources from which the sets were derived,
as well as the means, are different. Architectural and historical research treated those resources subject to their respective form of inquiry. Only archaeology investigated resources beneath the floor of
the basement. Foundations may have had the frame which they support
altered, even replaced. The authors of documents may record only to
have their products misplaced or destroyed; they may neglect, or rele-
gate, events to levels of insignificance; and they may purposefully
distort or mislead. The point is that the sets of dates are distinct
in that they are from different kinds of resources and derived by different methods of inquiry. By interpreting both sets, perhaps someone
will confirm or refute one or both with new evidence or new approaches.

2. Evidence of the original framed floor in Rooms A-9/10 should be interpreted. These points should be addressed. One, no knowledge of this
resource was available prior to its discovery during archaeological
investigation. Information about the Toombs House exists in more than
one form. Knowledge from all forms is important to understanding and
interpreting the house. Two, archaeological evidence demonstrates
that the same floor surface framed for in A-10 occurred in A-9 as
well, suggesting a single room originally. Three, the area of Room
A-9/10 was probably enclosed from the time foundations were built.
Dates derived from analysis of ceramics collected from footing and
joist trenches spread over less than two years. A framed floor would
require protection from climatic elements. Four, the area of the
house represented by A-9/10 was added to A-4/5/6. The main living
floor of A-9/10 was made to correspond with the main floor of A-4/5/6,
reducing ceiling height in A-9/10. The original floor of A-9/10 was

framed with its joists recessed in trenches to obtain ceiling height.
Five, the original function of this space is unknown.

Suggestions for Additional Research

As this archaeology at the Toombs House was delimited by funding, sche-
duled by restoration priorities, oriented by interpretive needs, and restricted
to the basement, a number of tracts of research could not be pursued. They
will be presented here in the hope that at some future date pursuit may be undertaken. The order of presentation is not one of priority.

1. Artifacts recovered from footing trenches and other associated features should be analyzed for the purpose of corroborating conclusions
   regarding the problem of determining season of construction. Trench
   configuration and placement alone are tenuous attributes on which to
   infer the season of an activity. This analysis would also help in assessing the validity of the assumptions made in defining this method
   of investigation.

2. Analysis of bone recovered from footing trenches and associated features should be undertaken in an attempt to discern patterns of diet
   and identify consumers. Answers should be sought to questions such as:
   What kinds of meat were eaten? Were the sources domestic, wild, or
   both? What cuts of meat were eaten? What butchering techniques were
   used? Can the consumers be identified as to function, as to race, as
   to numbers, or as to status? Can the season in which foundations were
   begun be determined by the presence or absence of certain kinds of
   meat?

3. If any archaeology is conducted outside of the basement of the Toombs
   House, one of its objectives should be finding the original site of

the Abbot house. Tendered on a single secondary historical reference
and some architectural indications was the possibility that a portion
of the Toombs House had been relocated. Supposedly, the Abbot portion
(A-4/5/6/7) was moved back from the road, which was implied to be the
street now fronting the house, East Robert Toombs Avenue. This problem of relocation was formed as a hypothesis for directing archaeological research. From archaeological results, which were interpreted
in the context of preceding research, a conclusion was drawn. The
Abbot portion (A-4/5/6/7) of the Toombs House had been relocated. As
this archaeology was restricted to the Toombs House, a new problem
arose. The location of the original site is unknown.

4. Archaeology conducted during the restoration of the Toombs House was
   restricted to the area of the basement. None of the outbuildings nor
   any of the yard was investigated. For a meaningful interpretation of
   the house and its residents, these resources cannot be ignored. As
   development of the site proceeds, whether in the form of restoring
   outbuildings, recreating landscapes, or providing visitor access, archaeological resources outside the basement must be addressed in all
   planning. No modification of the surface of the ground anywhere on
   the Toombs House property should occur without an archaeological assessment, the results of which should be a statement of potential for
   the occurrence of archaeological resources and their significance in
   a context of management recommendations. Such recommendations may be
   expected to range from 'no resources, therefore, no effect" to "significant resources, adverse effect, therefore, archaeological excavation for purpose of data recovery."

5. Archaeologically recovered ceramic artifacts should be reassembled

where possible, recording the room, excavation unit, and layer of origin for each fragment. The purposes are as follows: One, original
ceramic analysis would receive feedback as to the efficacy of South's
Mean Ceramic Dating Formula as well as the analysis itself. This procedure assumes larger forms are more accurately identifiable. Two,
the number of, type of, and presence of forms might assist with identifying the original, or previous, function of rooms. Three, reassembled items, with the location of each component known, might reflect
some of the manner of deposition. Were these ceramic items deposited
beneath the Toombs House because they were mislaid, damaged, out of
date, etc.? The completeness of the assemblage in conjunction with
the depositional origin of components may be informative about patterns of deposition and the behavior behind them.

REFERENCES CITED

Atwood, Wallace W.
  1940 The Physiographic Provinces of North America. Boston: Ginn and Com-
        pany.

Avery, I.W.
  1881 The History of the State of Georgia from 1850 to 1881. New York:
        Brown and Derby, Publishers.

Badzinski, Stanley, Jr.
  1972 Carpentry in Residential Construction. Englewood Cliffs, New Jersey:
        Prentice-Hall, Inc.

Bartram, William
  1792 (1973) Travels through North and South Carolina, Georgia, East and
        West Florida. Savannah: The Beehive Press.

  1943 Travels in Georgia and Florida, 1773-74: A Report to Dr. John Fother-
        gill. Annotated by Francis Harper. Transactions of the American Philo-
        sophical Society, n.s. 33, Pt. 2.

Belcher, John C.
  1964 The Dynamics of Georgia's Population. Monograph No. 12, The Social
        Science Research Institute and The Institute of Community and Area Devel-
        opment, University of Georgia, Athens.

Bonner, James C.
  1964 A History of Georgia Agriculture, 1732-1860. Athens: University of
        Georgia Press.

Bowen, Eliza A.
  1950 The Story of Wilkes County, Georgia. Marietta, Georgia: Continental
        Book Company.

Brender, E.V.
  1974 Impact of past land use of the lower piedmont forest. Journal of For-
        estry 72(1):34-6.

Bryant, Pat, compiler
  1977 Georgia Counties: Their Changing Boundaries. Georgia Surveyor Gen-
        eral Department, Office of the Secretary of State, Atlanta.

Buchanan, Paul E.
  1976 The Eighteenth-Century Frame Houses of Tidewater Virginia. In Build-
        ing Early America, edited by Charles E. Peterson, pp. 54-73. Radnor,
        Pennsylvania: Chilton Book Company.

Buckingham, James Silk
  1842 (1968) The Slave States of America, Vol. 1. New York: Negro Universi-
        ties Press.

Bunge, Mario
1967 Scientific Research I: The Search for System. New York: Springler-Verlag New York, Inc.

Callaway, James Etheridge
1948 The Early Settlement of Georgia. Athens: University of Georgia Press.

Candler, Allen D., compiler
1904 The Colonial Records of the State of Georgia, 1732-1752. Vol. 1. Atlanta: Franklin Printing and Publishing Company.

1904 The Minutes of the Common Council of the Trustees for Establishing the Colony of Georgia in America. The Colonial Records of the State of Georgia, 1732-1752, Vol. 2. Atlanta: Franklin Printing and Publishing Company.

1937 Letter Books of the Trustees, Vols. 10 and 11, 1745-1752. The Colonial Records of the State of Georgia, Vol. 31. Georgia Department of Archives and History, Atlanta. Typewritten.

Carrillio, Richard F.
1972 Exploratory excavations at Fort Hawkins, Macon, Georgia. In The Conference on Historic Site Archaeology Paper 1971. Vol. 6, pp. 51-68. Stanley South, editor.

Clark, William Z., Jr., and Arnold C. Zisa
1976 Physiographic Map of Georgia. (1:2,000,000) Geologic and Water Resources Division, Georgia Department of Natural Resources, Atlanta.

Cleland, Charles E., and James E. Fitting
1968 The crisis of identity: theory in historic sites archaeology. The Conference on Historic Site Archaeology Papers 1967. 2(2):124-38. Stanley South, editor.

Coleman, Kenneth
1960 Georgia History in Outline. Athens: University of Georgia Press.

1976 Colonial Georgia. New York: Charles Scribner's Sons.

1977 A History of Georgia. Athens: University of Georgia Press.

Cooper, Walter G.
1938 The Story of Georgia. 4 vols. New York: The American Historical Society, Inc.

Corkran, David H.
1962 The Cherokee Frontier. Norman: University of Oklahoma Press.

Corry, John Pitts
1936 Indian Affairs in Georgia, 1732-1756. Ph.D. Dissertation, University of Pennsylvania, Philadelphia.

Coulter, E. Merton
1960 Georgia, A Short History. Revised edition. Chapel Hill: University of North Carolina Press.

Coulter, E. Merton
1965 Old Petersburg and the Broad River Valley of Georgia. Athens: University of Georgia Press.

Crane, Verner W.
1929 The Southern Frontier, 1670-1732. Ann Arbor: University of Michigan Press.

Crispin, Frederic Swing
1942 Dictionary of Technical Terms. Milwaukee: The Bruce Publishing Company.

Curtis, John Obed
1979 Moving Historic Buildings. Technical Preservation Services Division, H.C.R.S., U.S. Department of Interior, Washington, D.C.

Dalzell, J. Ralph, and Gilbert Townsend
1954 Bricklaying: Skill and Practice. 2nd Ed. Revised. Chicago: American Technical Society.

DeBaillou, Clemens
1954 The White House in Augusta. Early Georgia 1(3):10-2.

DeVorsey, Louis, Jr.
1961 The Indian Boundary in the Southern Colonies, 1763-1775. Chapel Hill: University of North Carolina Press.

1971 Early maps as a source in the reconstruction of southern Indian landscapes. In Red, White, and Black, edited by Charles M. Hudson, pp. 12-30. Athens: University of Georgia Press.

Dietz, Albert G.H.
1974 Dwelling House Construction. 4th edition. Cambridge: M.I.T. Press.

Dollar, Clyde D.
1968 Some thoughts on theory and method in historical archaeology. The Conference on Historic Site Archaeology Papers 1967. 2(2):3-30. Stanley South, editor.

1971 More thoughts on theory and method in historical archaeology. The Conference on Historic Site Archaeology Papers 1969. 4(1):83-94. Stanley South, editor.

Downing, Andrew J.
1850 (1969) The Architecture of Country Houses. New York: Dover Publications, Inc.

1967 Cottage Residences, Rural Architecture and Landscape Gardening. Watkins Glen, New York: American Life Foundation.

Dunbar, Seymour
1937 A History of Travel in America. New York: Tudor Publishing Company.

Earle, Alice M.
  1900 (1969) Stage-Coach and Tavern Days. New York: Dover Publications,
     Inc.

Fant, H.B.
  1931 The Indian trade policy of the Trustees for establishing the colony of
     Georgia in America. Georgia Historical Quarterly 15(3):207-22.

Featherstonhaugh, G.W.
  1847 A Canoe Voyage Up the Minnay Sotor, Vol. 1. London: Richard Bentley.

Fenneman, Nevin M.
  1938 Physiography of Eastern United States. New York: McGraw-Hill Book
     Company, Inc.

Garrow, Patrick H.
  1979 Archaeological Considerations. In The Rock House, McDuffie County,
     Georgia, Norman Askins, pp. 19-33. The Wrightsboro Quaker Community
     Foundation, Inc., Thomson, Georgia.

  1980 Archaeological Investigations of the Elisha Winn House, Gwinnett
     County, Georgia (S.S.I. Project #ES-1630). Soil Systems, Inc., Marietta,
     Georgia.

Gates, Paul W.
  1960 The Farmer's Age: Agriculture, 1815-1860, Vol. 3. The Economic His-
     tory of the United States, edited by Henry David, et al.

General Assembly of the State of Georgia
  1805 Acts of the General Assembly of the State of Georgia. Augusta:
     George F. Randolph.

  1821 Acts of the General Assembly of the State of Georgia. Milledgeville:
     Camak and Hines.

Georgia Department of Natural Resources
  1972 Wilkes County: Robert Toombs House, Inventory-Nomination Form. State
     Historic Preservation Office, Division of Parks, Recreation and Historic
     Sites, Atlanta.

Gibbs, James
  1728 (1968) A Book of Architecture. New York: Benjamin Blom, Inc.

Godwin, George
  1838 (1972) Hints on Construction: Addressed to Architectural Students.
     Architectural Magazine, Vol. 5, edited by J. C. Loudon, pp. 250-5.

Goff, John H.
  1956 Travel on the Primitive Ways. Georgia Review 10(2):210-21.

Golley, Frank B.
  1962 Mammals of Georgia: ,A Study of Their Distribution and Functional Role
     in the Ecosystem. Athens: University of Georgia Press.

Goodman, Louis J. and R.H. Karol
    1968 Theory and Practice of Foundation Engineering. New York: The Macmil-
    lan Company.

Graham, Frank D.
    1924 Audel's Mason's and Builder's Guide #2. Indianapolis, Indiana: Theo-
    don Audel and Company.

Green, Fletcher M.
    1938 Georgia's Board of Public Works, 1817-1826. Georgia Historical Quar-
    terly 22(2):117-137.

Greene, Evarts B. and Virginia D. Harrington
    1966 American Population Before the Federal Census of 1790. Gloucester,
    Massachusetts: Peter Smith.

Gresham, Thomas H., Roy Doyon, and W. Dean Wood
    1981 Cultural Resources Reconnaissance of the Proposed Factory Shoals Wil-
    derness Park, Newton County, Georgia. Southeastern Wildlife Services,
    Inc., Athens, Georgia.

Halfpenny, William
    1725 (1968) The Art of Sound Building. New York: Benjamin Blom, Inc.

    1730 (1968) Practical Architecture. New York: Benjamin Blom, Inc.

Harper, Francis, editor
    1958 Travels of William Bartram, Naturalist's Edition. New Haven: Yale
    University Press.

Harrington, J.C.
    1955 Archeology as auxiliary to American history. American Anthropologist
    55(6):1121-30.

Harris, Cyril M., editor
    1975 Dictionary of Architecture and Construction. New York: McGraw-Hill
    Book Company.

Hawes, Lilla Mills, editor
    1963 The Frontiers of Georgia in the Late Eighteenth Century: Jonas Fauche
    to Joseph Vallance Bevan. Georgia Historical Quarterly 47(1):84-95.

Hawkins, Benjamin
    1848 (1971) A sketch of the Creek country. Collections of the Georgia His-
    torical Society, Vol. 3, Pt. 1. New York: Kraus Reprint Company.

Historic American Buildings Survey
    1941 National.Park Service, U.S. Department of Interior. Washington: U.S.
    Government Printing Office.

The History Group, Inc.
    1980 Historical Investigations of the Richard B. Russell Multiple Resource
    Area. Heritage Conservation and Recreation Service, Inter-agency Archaeo-
    logical Services, Atlanta.

Hitz, Alex M.
    1956 The Earliest Settlements in Wilkes County. Savannah: Georgia Histori-
          cal Society.

Hool, George A.
    1913 Reinforced Concrete Construction. New York: McGraw-Hill Book Com-
          pany, Inc.

Howell, Clark
    1926 History of Georgia. Chicago: The S.J. Clarke Publishing Company.

Hudson, Charles
    1976 The Southeastern Indians. Knoxville: University of Tennessee Press.

Hunt, Charles B.
    1967 Physiography of the United States. San Francisco: W.H. Freeman and
          Company.

Ivers, Larry E.
    1974 British Drums on the Southern Frontier. Chapel Hill: University of
          North Carolina Press.

Jeane, Donald G.
    1974 The Culture History of Grist Milling in Northwest Georgia. Unpublished
          Ph.D. dissertation, Department of Geography and Anthropology, Louisiana
          State University.

Johnson, Amanda
    1938 Georgia as Colony and State. Atlanta: Cherokee Publishing Company.
          Reprinted 1970.

Jones, George Fenwick
    1965 Von Reck's Second Report from Georgia. William and Mary Quarterly
          22(2):319-33.

Kaplan, Abraham
    1964 The Conduct of Inquiry. San Francisco: Chandler Publishing Company.

Kappler, Charles J., compiler and editor
    1904 Laws and Treaties: Indian Affairs, Vol. 2 (Treaties). Washington,
          D.C.: U.S. Government Printing Office.

Kelly, A.R.
    1938-39 The Macon Trading Post. American Antiquity 4:328-33.

Kelso, William M.
    1971 Historical Archaeology in Georgia, 1968: Two Nineteenth Century Sites.
          In The Conference on Historic Site Archaeology, Papers 1969, Vol. 4, pp.
          16-25. Stanley South, editor.

Kidder, Frank E., and Harry Parker
    1956 Architect's and Builder's Handbook. 18th Ed. New York: John Wiley
          and Sons, Inc.

King, Edward
1875 (1969) The Great South. New York: Burt Franklin. 2 vols.

Knight, Lucian Lamar
1917 A Standard History of Georgia and Georgians. Chicago: The Lewis Publishing Company.

Kroeber, A.L.
1938 (1963) Cultural and Natural Areas of Native North America. Berkeley
and Los Angeles: University of California Press.

Lafever, Minard
1833 (1969) The Modern Builder's Guide. New York: Dover Publications, Inc.

LaForge, Laurence
1925 The Central Upland. In Physical Geography of Georgia, Bulletin 42:
57-92. Geological Survey of Georgia. Atlanta.

Lamar, Lucius Quintus Cincinnatus
1821 A Compilation of the Laws of the State of Georgia, 1810-1819. Augusta:
T.S. Hannon.

Lane, Mills, editor
1973 The Rambler in Georgia: Traveller's Accounts of Frontier Georgia.
Savannah: The Beehive Press.

Langley, Batty
1727 (1971) The Builder's Chest-Book. Farnborough, England: Gregg International Publishers Limited.

1746 (1970) The Builder's Director or Bench-Mate. New York: Benjamin Blom,
Inc.

1750 (1967) The City and Country Builder's and Workman's Treasury of De-
signs. New York: Reissued by Benjamin Blom, Inc.

Langley, Batty, and Thomas Langley
1757 (1970) The Builder's Jewel. New York: Re-issued by Benjamin Blom,
Inc.

Linley, John
1972 Architecture of Middle Georgia. Athens: University of Georgia Press.

Logan, John Henry
1859 A History of the Upper Country of South Carolina, Vol. 1. Charleston:
S.G. Courtenay and Company.

Long, David D.
1916 Soil Survey of Wilkes County, Georgia. U.S. Department of Agriculture.
Washington, D.C.: U.S. Government Printing Office.

Loudon, J.D., compiler
1839 An Encyclopedia of Cottage, Farm, and Villa Architecture and Furniture.
London: Longman, Orme, Brown, Green, and Longmans.

McCall, Hugh
1784 (1969) The History of Georgia. Atlanta: Cherokee Publishing Company.

McCarthy, David F.
1977 Essentials of Soil Mechanics and Foundations. Reston, Virginia: Reston Publishing Company, Inc.

McElreath, Walter
1912 A Treatise on the Constitution of Georgia. Atlanta: The Harrison Company.

McKee, Harley J.
1973 Introduction to Early American Masonry. Washington, D.C.: National Trust for Historic Preservation in the United States.

Maldon, Leo D.
1977 How to Build with Stone, Brick, Concrete, and Tile. Blue Ridge Summit, Pennsylvania: Tab Books.

Marbury, Horatio, and William H. Crawford
1802 Digest of the Laws of the State of Georgia, From 1755 to 1800. Savannah: Seymour, Woolhopter and Stebbins.

Mereness, Newton D., editor
1961 Travels in the American Colonies. New York: Antiquarian Press, Ltd.

Mistovich, Timothy, and Roy Blair, Jr.
1979 Archaeological Investigations at Overlook Mansion, Macon, Georgia. Cultural Resource Services, Inc., Marietta, Georgia.

Morrison, Hugh S.
1952 Early American Architecture. New York: Oxford University Press.

Morse, Jedidiah
1797 The American Gazetteer. Boston: S. Hall, and Thomas and Andrews.

Moxon, Joseph
1703 (1970) Mechanick Exercises. New York: Praeger Publishers.

Myer, William E.
1928 Indian trails of the Southeast. 42nd Annual Report of the Bureau of American Ethnology, 1924-1925, pp. 727-857.

Neal, Ed
1976 Specifications for Job No. 7406, Restoration of the Robert Toombs House, Washington, Georgia. Columbus, Georgia: Biggers-Scarbrough-Neal-Crisp and Clark, Architects and Engineers.

1981 Personal Communication, March 24.

Neve, Richard
1726 (1969) The City and Country Purchaser and Builder's Dictionary. 2nd Edition. New York: Augustus M. Kelley, Publishers.

Newton, Milton B., Jr.
1970 Route geography and the routes of St. Helena Parish, Louisiana. An-
nals, Association of American Geographers 60(1):134-152.

1974 Cultural preadaptation and the upland South. In Geoscience and Man.
Edited by Bob F. Perkins, pp. 143-54.

Nichols, Frederick Doveton
1957 The Early Architecture of Georgia. Chapel Hill: University of North
Carolina Press.

1976 The Architecture of Georgia. Savannah: The Beehive Press.

Noel Hume, Ivor
1969 Historical Archaeology. New York: Alfred A. Knopf.

1970 A Guide to Artifacts of Colonial America. New York: Alfred A. Knopf.

Owsley, Frank L.
1945 The Pattern of Migration and Settlement on the Southern Frontier.
Journal of Southern History 11(2):147-176.

Pain, William
1762 (1972) The Builder's Companion and Workman's General Assistant. Westmead, England: Gregg International Publishers Limited.

Phillips, Ulrich B.
1905 Transportation in the Ante-Bellum South: An Economic Analysis. Quar-
terly Journal of Economics 19:434-51 (May). Boston: George H. Ellis
Company.

1908 A History of Transportation in the Eastern Cotton Belt to 1860. New
York: Columbia University Press.

1913 The Life of Robert Toombs. New York: The Macmillan Company.

Plummer, Gayther L.
1975 18th century forests in Georgia. Bulletin of Georgia Academy of Science 33(1):1-19.

Pope, John
1792 (1979) A Tour Through the Southern and Western Territories of the
United States of North America. Gainesville: University Presses of Florida.

Pownall, Thomas
1776 (1949) Topographical Description . . . of America. Pittsburgh: University of Pittsburgh Press.

Purdie, Hazel, compiler
1979 Georgia Bibliography: County History. Reader Services, Division of
Public Library Services, Georgia Department of Education, Atlanta.

Putnam, R.E., and G.E. Carlson
1974 Architectural and Building Trades Dictionary. Chicago: American
Technical Society, 3rd Edition, 12th printing.

Ramsey, Robert W.
1964 Carolina Cradle: Settlement of the Northwest Carolina Frontier, 1747-
      1762. Chapel Hill: University of North Carolina Press.

Ray, J. Edgar
1961 The Art of Bricklaying. Peoria, Illinois: Charles A. Bennett Company.

Ready, Milton LaVerne
1970 An Economic History of Colonial Georgia, 1732-1754. Ph.D. disserta-
      tion, University Microfilms, Ann Arbor.

Reap, James K.
1977 Historic Structures Field Survey: Wilkes County, 3 vols. Historic
      Preservation Section, Georgia Department of Natural Resources, Atlanta.

Rights, Douglas L.
1931 The trading path to the Indians. North Carolina Historical Review 8:
      403-26.

Robinson, William
1733 (1968) Proportional Architecture. Farnborough, England: Gregg Inter-
      national Publishers Limited.

Rogers, Ava D.
1971 The Housing of Oglethorpe County, Georgia, 1790-1860. Tallahassee:
      Florida State University Press.

Rothrock, Mary U.
1929 Carolina traders among the Overhill Cherokees, 1690-1760. East Tennes-
      see Historical Society's Publications 1:3-18.

Salmon, William
1734 (1969) Palladio Londinensis: or the London Art of Building. Westmead,
      England: Gregg International Publishers Limited.

Saye, Albert B., editor
1942 Georgia's Charter of 1732. Athens: University of Georgia Press.

Schuyler, Robert L.
1977 The written word, the spoken word, observed behavior and preserved be-
      havior: the various contexts available to the archaeologists. The Con-
      ference on Historic Site Archaeology Papers 1975 10(2):99-120. Stanley
      South, editor.

Seakins, L.W., and S. Smith
1965 Practical Brickwork. New York: Chemical Publishing Company, Inc.

Shelford, Victor E.
1963 The Ecology of North America. Urbana: University of Illinois Press.

Smith, Bruce D.
1978 Prehistoric Patterns of Human Behavior. New York: Academic Press.

South, Stanley, editor
1968 Historical archaeology forum on theory and method in historical archaeology. The Conference on Historic Site Archaeology Papers 1967 2(2):1-188.

1972 Evolution and horizon as revealed in ceramic analysis in historical archaeology. The Conference on Historic Site Archaeology Papers 6:71-116. Stanley South, editor.

1974 Palmetto Parapets. Anthropological Studies 1. Occasional Papers of the Institute of Archaeology and Anthropology, University of South Carolina, Columbia.

1977 Method and Theory in Historical Archaeology. New York: Academic Press.

Sowers, George B., and George F. Sowers
1961 Introductory Soil Mechanics and Foundations. New York: Macmillan Company.

Spalding, Phinizy
1977 Colonial Period. In A History of Georgia. Edited by Kenneth Coleman. University of Georgia Press, Athens.

State of Georgia
n.d. Georgia Official and Statistical Register, 1973-1974. Department of Archives and History, Office of the Secretary of State, Atlanta.

Stoddard, Ralph P.
1946 Brick Structures. New York: McGraw-Hill Book Company, Inc.

Stovall, Pleasant A.
1892 Robert Toombs. New York: Cassell Publishing Company.

Suddeth, Ruth Elgin, I.L. Osterhout, and G.L. Hutcheson
1966 Empire Builders of Georgia. 4th Edition. Austin, Texas: Steck-Vaughn Company.

Swanton, John R.
1946 The Indians of the Southeastern United States. Smithsonian Institution, Bureau of American Ethnology, Bulletin 137. Washington, D.C.

Tarver, James D.
1958 Migration in Georgia. College of Agriculture Experiment Stations, Research Report 26 (May). University of Georgia, Athens.

Taylor, George Rogers
1951 The Transportation Revolution, 1815-1860. Vol. 4 of The Economic History of the United States. Edited by Henry David, et al. White Plains, New York: M.E. Sharpe, Inc.

Thomas, Kenneth H., Jr.
1974 The Robert Toombs House. Historic Preservation Section, Georgia Department of Natural Resources, Atlanta.

Thompson, M.T.
    1950 The Potamophilous Indian, The Historic Role of the Rivers of Georgia.
    Georgia Mineral Society Newsletter 3(3):84-90.

    1954 Finaletto, The Historic Role of the Rivers of Georgia. Georgia Mineral Society Newsletter 7(2):61-70.

Thompson, William Y.
    1966 Robert Toombs of Georgia. Baton Rouge: Louisiana State University
    Press.

Thornbury, William D.
    1965 Regional Geomorphology of the United States. New York: John Wiley
    and Sons, Inc.

Tweney, C.F., and L.E.C. Hughes, editors
    1942 Chamber's Technical Dictionary. New York: The Macmillan Company.

Ulrey, Harry F.
    1970 Carpenters and Builders Library No. 3. 3rd edition. Indianapolis,
    Indiana: Howard W. Sams and Company.

U.S. Department of Agriculture
    1941 Climate and Man. Yearbook of Agriculture. Washington, D.C.

U.S. Department of the Navy
    1972 Basic Construction Techniques. New York: Dover Publications, Inc.

Van Der Schalie, Henry, and Paul W. Parmalee
    1960 Animals Remains from the Etowah Site, Mound C, Bartow County, Georgia.
    Florida Anthropologist 13(2-3):37-54.

Vassar, Rena, editor
    1961 Some Short Remarks on the Indian Trade in the Charikees and in the Man-
    agement thereof since the Year 1977. Ethnohistory 8:401-23.

Vollmer, Ernst
    1967 Encyclopedia of Hydraulics, Soil and Foundation Engineering. New York:
    Elsevier Publishing Company.

Volney, C.F.
    1804 (1968) A View of the Soil and Climate of the United States of America.
    New York: Hafner Publishing Company, Inc.

Wagner, Willis H.
    1969 Modern Carpentry. South Holland, Illinois: The Goodheart-Willcox Com-
    pany, Inc.

Walker, Iain C.
    1967 Historic archaeology methods and principles. Historical Archaeology
    1:23-33.

    1968 Comment on Clyde Dollar's 'Some Thoughts on Theory and Method in His-
    torical Archaeology.' The Conference on Historic Site Archaeology Papers
    1967. 2(2):105-23).

Walker, Iain C.
   1970   The crisis of identity-history and anthropology. The Conference on
          Historic Site Archaeology Papers 1968. 3:62-9. Stanley South, editor.

Watkins, Robert, and George Watkins
   1800   A Digest of the Laws of the State of Georgia to 1798. Philadelphia,
          Pennsylvania: R. Aitken.

Weaver, David Charles
   1972   The Transport Expansion Sequence in Georgia and the Carolinas, 1670-
          1900: A Search for Spatial Regularities. Ph.D. dissertation, University
          of Florida. University Microfilms, Ann Arbor.

Wharton, Charles H.
   1977   The Natural Environments of Georgia. Office of Planning and Research,
          Georgia Department of Natural Resources, Atlanta.

White, George
   1849   Statistics of the State of Georgia. Savannah: W. Thorne Williams.

   1854   Historical Collections of Georgia. New York: Pudney and Russell, Pub-
          lishers.

Wilkes County, Georgia
   MS   Deeds, Book CC:167. On microfilm reel 43-30 , Georgia Department of Ar-
        chives and History, Atlanta.

   MS   Deeds, Book QQ:243. On microfilm reel 43-37, Georgia Department of Ar-
        chives and History, Atlanta.

   MS   Deeds, Book RR:295. On microfilm reel 43-37, Georgia Department of Ar-
        chives and History, Atlanta.

   MS   Deeds, Book RR:298. On microfilm reel 43-37, Georgia Department of Ar-
        chives and History, Atlanta.

   MS   Deeds, Book XX:227. On microfilm reel 43-40, Georgia Department of Ar-
        chives and History, Atlanta.

   MS   Deeds, Book XX:408. On microfilm reel 43-40, Georgia Department of Ar-
        chives and History, Atlanta.

Willingham, Robert Marion, Jr.
   1969   We Have This Heritage. Wilkes Publishing Company.

Wilms, Douglas C.
   1973   Cherokee Indian Land Use in Georgia, 1800-1838. Unpublished Ph.D. dis-
          sertation, University of Georgia, Athens.

Wood, Karen G.
   1980a Archaeological Investigations at the Crawford W. Long House, Daniels-
          ville, Georgia. Southeastern Wildlife Services, Inc., Athens, Georgia.

Wood, Karen G.
    1980[b] Archaeological Investigations at the Thomas M. Gilmer Site, Ogle-
        thorpe County, Georgia. Southeastern Wildlife Services, Inc. Athens,
        Georgia.

Wood, W. Dean
    1979 Archaeological Investigations at the Historic Site of Twin Oaks,
        Meriwether County, Georgia. Southeastern Wildlife Services, Inc.,
        Athens, Georgia.

    1980 Archaeological Investigations at the Bledsoe-Greene House, Eatonton,
        Georgia. Southeastern Wildlife Services, Inc. Athens, Georgia.

Writers' Program of the Work Projects Administration.
    1941 The Story of Washington-Wilkes. Athens: University of Georgia Press.

Zelinsky, Wilbur
    1951 An Isochronic Map of Georgia Settlement, 1750-1850. Georgia Histor-
        ical Quarterly 35(3):191-5.

    1954 The Greek Revival house in Georgia. Journal of the Society of Arch-
        itectural Historians 13(2):9-12.

APPENDIX

APPENDIX

Toombs House 1976

Applications of the Mean Ceramic Date Formula (South 1972)

Ceramic type no.	Ceramic type name	Median date	Sherd count	Product
	Room A-1, total ceramic assemblage*			
7	Overglaze enamelled China trade porcelain	1808	27	48,816
29	"Jackfield" ware	1706	3	5,280
2	Whiteware	1860	1	1,860
9	Embossed feathers, fish scales, etc., on pearlware	1810	1	1,810
14	"Annular wares" creamware	1798	1	1,798
15	Lighter yellow creamware	1798	29	52,142
23	Transfer-printed creamware	1790	3	5,370
17	Underglaze blue handpainted pearlware	1800	2	3,600
4	Underglaze polychrome pearlware....	1830	4	7,320
19	Blue and green edged pearlware	1805	9	16,245
11	Transfer-printed pearlware	1818	61	110,898
20	Undecorated pearlware	1805	47	84,835
13	"Annular wares" pearlware	1805	11	19,855
			199	359,829

Mean ceramic date = 359,829 ÷ 199 = 1808.2

Sherd count total: 234
Unidentified sherds: 35
Percentage identified: 85

	Room A-1, unit E1N1, footing trench			
17	Underglaze blue handpainted pearlware	1800	1	1,800
4	Underglaze polychrome pearlware....	1830	1	1,830
20	Undecorated pearlware	1805	1	1,805
			3	5,435

Mean ceramic date = 5,435 ÷ 3 = 1811.7

Sherd count total: 3
Unidentified sherds: 0
Percentage identified: 100

* Throughout, contents of footing trenches were considered with the rooms to which the trenches pertained.

APPENDIX

Toombs House 1976

Applications of the Mean Ceramic Date Formula (South 1972)

Ceramic type no.	Ceramic type name	Median date	Sherd count	Product
	Room A-1, hearth fill			
15	Lighter yellow creamware	1798	1	1,798
11	Transfer-printed pearlware	1818	2	3,636
20	Undecorated pearlware	1805	1	1,805
7	Overglaze enamelled China trade porcelain	1808	1	1,808
			5	9,047

Mean ceramic date = 9,047 ÷ 5 = 1809.4

Sherd count total: 5
Unidentified sherds: 0
Percentage identified: 100

	Room A-1, unit E1N2, construction layer			
15	Lighter yellow creamware	1798	5	8,990
17	Underglaze blue handpainted pearlware	1800	1	1,800
19	Blue and green edged pearlware	1805	2	3,610
11	Transfer-printed pearlware	1818	6	10,908
20	Undecorated pearlware	1805	4	7,220
			18	32,528

Mean ceramic date = 32,528 ÷ 18 = 1807.1

Sherd count total: 24
Unidentified sherds: 6
Percentage identified: 75

	Room A-2, total ceramic assemblage			
15	Lighter yellow creamware	1798	16	28,768
4	Underglaze polychrome pearlware....	1830	4	7,320
19	Blue and green edged pearlware	1805	17	30,685
9	Embossed feathers, fish cales, etc....	1810	2	3,620
11	Transfer-printed pearlware	1818	50	90,900
20	Undecorated pearlware	1805	59	106,495
10	"Willow" transfer-pattern on pearlware	1818	9	16,362
13	"Annular wares" pearlware	1805	1	1,805
6	Mocha	1843	1	1,843
			159	287,798

APPENDIX

Toombs House 1976

Applications of the Mean Ceramic Date Formula (South 1972)

Ceramic type no.	Ceramic type name	Median date	Sherd count	Product

Mean ceramic date = 287,798 ÷ 159 = 1810.1

Sherd count total: 179
Unidentified sherds: 20
Percentage identified: 89

Room A-2, unit E4N1, footing trench

15	Lighter yellow creamware	1798	1	1,798
19	Blue and green edged pearlware	1805	1	1,805
20	Undecorated pearlware	1805	1	1,805
			3	5,408

Mean ceramic date = 5,408 ÷ 3 = 1802.7

Sherd county total: 3
Unidentified sherds: 0
Percentage identified: 100

Room A-2, unit W17.8S0, exterior footing trench

15	Lighter yellow creamware	1798	1	1,798
4	Underglaze polychrome pearlware....	1830	1	1,830
11	Transfer-printed pearlware	1818	2	3,636
20	Undecorated pearlware	1805	1	1,805
			5	9,069

Mean ceramic date = 9,069 ÷ 5 = 1813.8

Sherd count total: 5
Unidentified sherds: 0
Percentage identified: 100

Room A-3, total ceramic assemblage

13	"Annular wares" pearlware	1805	2	3,610
11	Transfer-printed pearlware	1818	18	32,724

APPENDIX

Toombs House 1976

Applications of the Mean Ceramic Date Formula (South 1972)

Ceramic type no.	Ceramic type name	Median date	Sherd count	Product
20	Undecorated pearlware	1805	18	32,490
15	Lighter yellow creamware	1798	4	7,192
4	Underglaze polychrome pearlware....	1830	2	3,660
19	Blue and green edged pearlware	1805	1	1,805
			45	81,481

Mean ceramic date = 81,481 ÷ 45 = 1810.7

Sherd count total: 48
Unidentified sherds: 3
Percentage identified: 94

Room A-4/5/6, total ceramic assemblage

7	Overglaze enamelled China trade porcelain	1808	78	141,024
2	Whiteware	1860	3	5,580
78	Luster decorated wares	1815	8	14,520
15	Lighter yellow creamware	1798	397	713,806
17	Underglaze blue handpainted pearlware	1800	59	106,200
4	Underblaze polychrome pearlware....	1830	89	162,870
13	"Annular wares" pearlware	1805	103	185,915
19	Blue and green edged pearlware	1805	273	492,765
9	Embossed feathers, fish scales, etc., on pearlware	1810	22	39,820
11	Transfer-printed pearlware	1818	1120	2,036,160
20	Undecorated pearlware	1805	712	1,285,160
23	Transfer-printed creamware	1790	1	1,790
22	Creamware	1791	4	7,164
14	"Annular wares" creamware	1798	4	7,192
8	"Finger-painted" wares	1805	3	5,415
27	"Black basalts" stoneware	1785	1	1,785
36	"Clouded" wares, tortoise shell, mottled glazed cream-colored ware	1755	1	1,755
6	Mocha	1841	1	1,841
12	Underglaze polychrome pearlware	1805	2	3,610 .
			2881	5,214,372

Mean ceramic date: 5,214,372 ÷ 2,881 = 1809.9

Sherd count total: 3,973
Unidentified sherds: 1,115
Percentage identified: 72

APPENDIX

Toombs House 1976

Applications of the Mean Ceramic Date Formula (South 1972)

Ceramic type no.	Ceramic type name	Median date	Sherd count	Product
	Room A-4/5/6, unit E6.9N6.2, footing trench			
15	Lighter yellow creamware	1798	3	5,394
19	Blue and green edged pearlware	1805	2	3,610
11	Transfer-printed pearlware	1818	3	5,454
20	Undecorated pearlware	1805	3	5,415
			11	19,873

Mean ceramic date = 19,873 ÷ 11 = 1806.6

Sherd count total: 14
Unidentified sherds: 3
Percentage identified: 79

Ceramic type no.	Ceramic type name	Median date	Sherd count	Product
	Room A-4/5/6, unit E5.1N26.9, footing trench			
15	Lighter yellow creamware	1798	3	5,394
13	"Annular wares"	1805	1	1,805
11	Transfer-printed pearlware	1818	1	1,818
			5	9,017

Mean ceramic date = 9,017 ÷ 5 = 1803.4

Sherd count total: 5
Unidentified sherds: 0
Percentage identified: 100

Ceramic type no.	Ceramic type name	Median date	Sherd count	Product
	Room A-4/5/6, unit E18.8N2.2, footing trench			
15	Lighter yellow creamware	1798	1	1,798
13	"Annular wares" pearlware	1805	1	1,805
19	Blue and green edged pearlware	1805	1	1,805
20	Undecorated pearlware	1805	3	5,415
			6	10,823

Mean ceramic date = 10,823 ÷ 6 = 1803.8

Sherd count total: 8
Unidentified sherds: 2
Percentage identified: 75

APPENDIX

Toombs House 1976

Applications of the Mean Ceramic Date Formula (South 1972)

Ceramic type no.	Ceramic type name	Median date	Sherd count	Product
	Room A-4/5/6, unit E19.25N17.35, footing trench			
11	Transfer-printed pearlware	1818	5	9,090
20	Undecorated pearlware	1805	1	1,805
			6	10,895

Mean ceramic date = 10,895 ÷ 6 = 1815.8

Sherd count total: 7
Unidentified sherds: 1
Percentage identified: 86

	Room A-4/5/6, unit E19.25N24.9, footing trench			
7	Overglaze enamelled China trade porcelain	1808	1	1,808
15	Lighter yellow creamware	1798	1	1,798
13	"Annular wares" pearlware	1805	1	1,805
11	Transfer-printed pearlware	1818	3	5,454
20	Undecorated pearlware	1805	1	1,805
			7	12,670

Mean ceramic date = 12,670 ÷ 7 = 1810

Sherd count total: 7
Unidentified sherds: 0
Percentage identified: 100

	Room A-4/5/6, unit W4.1S0 (outside), footing trench			
15	Lighter yellow creamware	1798	1	1,798
12	Underglaze polychrome pearlware	1805	1	1,805
19	Blue and green edged pearlware	1805	1	1,805
20	Undecorated pearlware	1805	3	5,415
			6	10,823

Mean ceramic date = 10,823 ÷ 6 = 1803.8

Sherd count total: 6
Unidentified sherds: 0
Percentage identified: 100

APPENDIX

Toombs House 1976

Applications of the Mean Ceramic Date Formula (South 1972)

Ceramic type no.	Ceramic type name	Median date	Sherd count	Product
	Room A-4/5/6, unit fourth layer of hearth fill			
7	Overglaze enamelled China trade porcelain	1808	2	3,616
15	Lighter yellow creamware	1798	2	3,596
17	Underglaze blue hand painted	1800	4	7,200
12	Underglaze polychrome pearlware	1805	1	1,805
13	"Annular wares" pearlware	1805	2	3,610
19	Blue and green edged pearlware	1805	2	3,610
9	Embossed feathers, fish scales, etc., on pearlware	1810	1	1,810
11	Transfer-printed pearlware	1818	7	12,726
20	Undecorated pearlware	1805	13	23,465
			34	61,438

Mean ceramic date = 61,438 ÷ 34 = 1807

Sherd count total: 40
Unidentified sherds: 6
Percentage identified: 90

From Room A-3, unit E3N7.73, footing trench on exterior of northeast pier of A-4/5/6

11	Transfer-printed pearlware	1818	2	3,636
			2	3,636

Mean ceramic date = 3,636 ÷ 2 - 1818

Sherd count total: 2
Unidentified sherds: 0
Percentage identified: 100

From Room A-7, unit E10.6N7.4, footing trench on exterior of southwest pier of A-4/5/6

15	Lighter yellow creamware	1808	7	12,656
36	"Clouded" wares, tortoise shell, mottled glazed....	1755	1	1,755
4	Underglaze polychrome pearlware, directly....	1830	1	1,830

APPENDIX

Toombs House 1976

Applications of the Mean Ceramic Date Formula (South 1972)

Ceramic type no.	Ceramic type name	Median date	Sherd count	Product
19	Blue and green edged pearlware	1805	5	9,025
11	Transfer-printed pearlware	1818	5	9,090
20	Undecorated pearlware	1805	4	7,220
			23	41,576

Mean ceramic date = 41,576 ÷ 23 = 1807.7

Sherd county total: 23
Unidentified sherds: 0
Percentage identified: 100

From Room A-7, unit E10.6N17.6, footing trench on exterior of central pier on west side of A-4/5/6

7	Overglaze enamelled China trade porclain	1808	1	1,808
15	Lighter yellow creamware	1798	18	32,364
4	Underglaze polychrome pearlware, directly....	1830	2	3,660
13	"Annular wares" pearlware	1805	1	1,805
6	Mocha	1843	1	1,843
19	Blue and green edged pearlware	1805	6	10,830
11	Transfer-printed pearlware	1818	30	54,540
			59	106,850

Mean ceramic date = 106,850 ÷ 59 = 1811.0

Sherd count total: 77
Unidentified sherds: 18
Percentage identified: 77

Room A-7, total ceramic assemblage

7	Overglaze enamelled Chinese trade porcelain	1808	18	32,544
15	Lighter yellow creamware	1798	270	485,460
17	Underglaze blue handpainted pearlware	1800	14	25,200
4	Underglaze polychrome pearlware....	1830	28	51,240
13	"Annular wares" pearlware	1805	40	72,200
19	Blue and green edged pearlware	1805	111	200,355
11	Transfer-printed pearlware	1818	316	574,488

APPENDIX

Toombs House 1976

Applications of the Mean Ceramic Date Formula (South 1972)

Ceramic type no.	Ceramic type name	Median date	Sherd count	Product
20	Undecorated pearlware	1805	288	519,840
1	Brown stoneware bottles for ink, beer, etc.	1860	1	1,860
36	"Clouded" wares, tortoise shell....	1755	1	1,755
78	Luster decorated wares	1815	1	1,815
6	Mocha	1843	2	3,686
			1090	1,970,443

Mean ceramic date = 1,970,443 ÷ 1,090 = 1807.7

Sherd count total: 1,426
Unidentified sherds: 336
Percentage identified: 76

Room A-7, unit E20.7N4, total of exterior unit

15	Lighter yellow creamware	1798	7	12,586
4	Underglaze polychrome pearlware....	1830	1	1,830
9	Embossed feathers, fish scales, etc., on pearlware	1810	1	1,810
11	Transfer-printed pearlware	1818	6	10,908
20	Undecorated pearlware	1805	5	9,025
			20	36,159

Mean ceramic date = 36,159 ÷ 20 = 1807.9

Sherd count total: 33
Unidentified sherds: 13
Percentage identified: 61

Room A-7, unit E20.7N4, exterior footing trench

15	Lighter yellow creamware	1798	3	5,394
20	Undecorated pearlware	1805	1	1,805
			4	7,199

Mean ceramic date = 7,199 ÷ 4 = 1799.7

Sherd count total: 6
Unidentified sherds: 2
Percentage identified: 67

APPENDIX

Toombs House 1976

Applications of the Mean Ceramic Date Formula (South 1972)

Ceramic type no.	Ceramic type name	Median date	Sherd count	Product
	Room A-7, unit E20.7N9, exterior footing trench			
15	Lighter yellow creamware	1798	4	7,192
17	Underglaze blue handpainted pearlware	1800	1	1,800
19	Blue and green edged pearlware	1805	1	1,805
11	Transfer-printed pearlware	1818	1	1,818
20	Undecorated pearlware	1805	3	5,415
			10	18,030

Mean ceramic date = 18,030 ÷ 10 = 1803

Sherd count total: 15
Unidentified·sherds: 5
Percentage identified: 67

	Room A-7, unit E7.6N2.6, footing trench			
7	Overglaze enamelled Chinese trade porcelain	1808	1	1,808
15	Lighter yellow creamware	1798	3	5,394
11	Transfer-printed pearlware	1818	3	5,454
20	Undecorated pearlware	1805	6	10,830
			13	23,486

Mean ceramic date = 23,486 ÷ 13 = 1806.6

Sherd count total: 15
Unidentified sherds: 2
Percentage identified: 87

	From Room A-8, unit E20N15.2, exterior footing trench			
15	Lighter yellow creamware	1798	2	3,596
13	"Annular wares" pearlware	1805	1	1,805
20	Undecorated pearlware	1805	1	1,805
			4	7,206

Mean ceramic date = 7,206 ÷ 4 = 1801.5

Sherd count total: 4
Unidentified sherds: 0
Percentage identified: 100

APPENDIX

Toombs House 1976

Applications of the Mean Ceramic Date Formula (South 1972)

Ceramic type no.	Ceramic type name	Median date	Sherd count	Product
	From Room A-8, unit E20N8.1, exterior footing trench			
20	Undecorated pearlware	1805	4	7,220
			4	7,220

Mean ceramic date = 7,220 ÷ 4 = 1805

Sherd count total: 5
Unidentified sherds: 1
Percentage identified: 80

	Room A-8, total ceramic assemblage			
7	Overglaze enamelled China trade porcelain	1808	3	5,424
15	Lighter yellow creamware	1798	12	21,576
17	Underglaze blue handpainted pearlware	1800	5	9,000
4	Underglaze polychrome pearlware	1830	2	3,660
19	Blue and green edged pearlware	1805	5	9,025
9	Embossed feathers, fish scales, etc., on pearlware	1810	1	1,810
11	Transfer-printed pearlware	1818	30	54,540
20	Undecorated pearlware	1805	8	14,440
13	"Annular wares" pearlware	1805	2	3,610
			68	123,085

Mean ceramic date = 123,085 ÷ 68 = 1810.1

Sherd count total: 98
Unidentified sherds: 30
Percentage identified: 69

	Room A-8, unit E10N2, exterior footing trench			
15	Lighter yellow creamware	1798	1	1,798
11	Transfer-printed pearlware	1818	4	7,272
20	Undecorated pearlware	1805	1	1,805
			6	10,875

Mean ceramic date = 10,875 ÷ 6 = 1812.5

APPENDIX

Toombs House 1976

Applications of the Mean Ceramic Date Formula (South 1972)

Ceramic type no.	Ceramic type name	Median date	Sherd count	Product
	Sherd count total: 6 Unidentified sherds: 0 Percentage identified: 100			
	Room A-8, unit E13N18.2, footing trench			
17	Underglaze blue handpainted pearlware	1800	1	1,800
15	Lighter yellow creamware	1798	2	3,596
13	"Annular wares" pearlware	1805	1	1,805
20	Undecorated pearlware	1805	4	7,220
			8	14,421

Mean ceramic date = 14,421 ÷ 8 = 1802.6

Sherd count total: 10
Unidentified sherds: 2
Percentage identified: 80

	Room A-9, total ceramic assemblage			
15	Lighter yellow creamware	1798	11	19,778
13	"Annular wares" pearlware	1805	1	1,805
19	Blue and green edged pearlware	1805	3	5,415
11	Transfer-printed pearlware	1818	10	18,180
20	Undecorated pearlware	1805	12	21,660
			37	66,838

Mean ceramic date = 66,838 ÷ 37 = 1806.4

Sherd count total: 37
Unidentified sherds: 4
Percentage identified: 90

	Room A-9, unit E1.5N2.5, footing trench			
15	Lighter yellow creamware	1798	4	7,192
13	"Annular wares" pearlware	1805	1	1,805

APPENDIX

Toombs House 1976

Applications of the Mean Ceramic Date Formula (South 1972)

Ceramic type no.	Ceramic type name	Median date	Sherd count	Product
19	Blue and green edged pearlware	1805	2	3,610
11	Transfer-printed pearlware	1818	3	5,454
20	Undecorated pearlware	1805	5	9,025
			15	27,086

Mean ceramic date = 27,086 ÷ 15 = 1805.7

Sherd count total: 17
Unidentified sherds: 2
Percentage identified: 88

Room A-9, unit E1.5N2.5, joist trench

11	Transfer-printed pearlware	1818	3	5,454
20	Undecorated pearlware	1805	1	1,805
			4	7,259

Mean ceramic date = 7,259 ÷ 4 = 1814.7

Sherd count total: 4
Unidentified sherds: 0
Percentage identified: 100

From Room A-3, footing trench on exterior of south wall of A-9

15	Lighter yellow creamware	1798	3	5,394
19	Blue and green edged pearlware	1805	1	1,805
20	Undecorated pearlware	1805	3	5,415
			7	12,614

Mean ceramic date = 12,614 ÷ 7 = 1802

Sherd count total: 7
Unidentified sherds: 0
Percentage identified: 100

APPENDIX

Toombs House 1976

Applications of the Mean Ceramic Date Formula (South 1972)

Room A-10, total ceramic assemblage

15	Lighter yellow creamware	1798	206	370,388
19	Blue and green edged pearlware	1805	36	64,980
11	Transfer-printed pearlware	1818	153	278,154
20	Undecorated pearlware	1805	157	283,385
4	Underglaze polychrome pearlware....	1830	10	18,300
7	Overglaze enamelled China trade porcelain	1808	19	34,352
17	Underglaze blue handpainted pearlware	1800	4	7,200
13	"Annular wares" pearlware	1805	18	32,490
9	Embossed feathers, fish scales, etc. on pearlware	1810	5	9,050
1	Brown stoneware bottles for ink, beer, etc.	1860	1	1,860
78	Luster decorated ware	1815	3	5,445
			612	1,105,604

Mean ceramic date = 1,105,604 $\div$ 612 = 1806.5

Sherd count total: 690
Unidentified sherds: 81
Percentage identified: 89

Room A-10, unit E2.2N3.4, footing trench on south wall

15	Lighter yellow creamware	1798	1	1,798
11	Transfer-printed pearlware	1818	1	1,818
20	Undecorated pearlware	1805	2	3,610
			4	7,226

Mean ceramic date = 7,226 $\div$ 4 = 1806.5

Sherd count total: 4
Unidentified sherds: 0
Percentage identified: 100

Room A-10, unit E2.2N3.4, footing trench on west wall

15	Lighter yellow creamware	1798	2	3,596
19	Blue and green edged pearlware	1805	1	1,805
11	Transfer-printed pearlware	1818	1	1,818
20	Undecorated pearlware	1805	2	3,610
			6	10,829.

APPENDIX

Toombs House 1976

Applications of the Mean Ceramic Date Formula (South 1972)

Mean ceramic date = 10,829 ÷ 6 = 1804.8

Sherd count total: 8
Unidentified sherds: 2
Percentage identified: 75

Room A-10, unit E6.95N8.8, footing trench

7	Overglaze enamelled China trade porcelain	1808	1	1,808
15	Lighter yellow creamware	1798	6	10,788
4	Underglaze polychrome pearlware....	1830	1	1,830
19	Blue and green edged pearlware	1805	1	1,850
9	Embossed feathers, fish scales, etc. on pearlware	1810	3	5,430
11	Transfer-printed pearlware	1818	3	5,454
20	Undecorated pearlware	1805	5	9,025
			20	36,185

Mean ceramic date = 36,185 ÷ 20 = 1809.2

Sherd count total: 27
Unidentified: 7
Percentage identified: 74

Room A-10, unit E18N16.9, footing trench

7	Overglaze enamelled China trade porcelain	1808	2	3,616
15	Lighter yellow creamware	1805	11	19,855
13	"Annular wares" pearlware	1805	2	3,610
19	Blue and green edged pearlware	1805	2	3,610
11	Transfer-printed pearlware	1818	11	19,998
20	Undecorated pearlware	1805	7	12,635
			35	63,324

Mean ceramic date = 63,324 ÷ 35 = 1809.3

Sherd count total: 37
Unidentified sherds: 2
Percentage identified: 95

APPENDIX

Toombs House 1976

Applications of the Mean Ceramic Date Formula (South 1972)

Ceramic type no.	Ceramic type name	Median date	Sherd count	Product
	Room A-10, E18N8.4, footing trench			
15	Lighter yellow creamware	1798	10	17,980
13	"Annular wares" pearlware	1805	1	1,805
19	Blue and green edged pearlware	1805	1	1,805
11	Transfer-printed pearlware	1818	8	14,544
20	Undecorated pearlware	1805	8	14,440
			28	50,574

Mean ceramic date = 50,574 ÷ 28 = 1806.2

Sherd count total: 33
Unidentified sherds: 5
Percentage identified: 85

Ceramic type no.	Ceramic type name	Median date	Sherd count	Product
	Room A-10, EON2.5, footing trench			
7	Overglaze enamelled China trade porcelain	1808	1	1,808
78	Luster decorated wares	1815	2	3,630
15	Lighter yellow creamware	1798	9	16,182
17	Underglaze blue handpainted pearlware	1800	3	5,400
4	Underglaze polychrome pearlware. . .	1830	1	1,830
19	Blue and green edged pearlware	1805	4	7,220
11	Transfer-printed pearlware	1818	16	29,088
20	Undecorated pearlware	1805	11	19,855
			47	85,013

Mean ceramic date = 85,013 ÷ 47 = 1808.8

Sherd count total: 48
Unidentified sherds: 1
Percentage identified: 98

Ceramic type no.	Ceramic type name	Median date	Sherd count	Product
	Room A-10, joist trenches (E6.95N8.8; E15.5N14.9; E17.7N14.9)			
15	Lighter yellow creamware	1798	23	41,354
4	Underglaze polychrome pearlware....	1830	2	3,660
11	Transfer-printed pearlware	1818	14	25,452
20	Undecorated pearlware	1805	22	39,710
7	Overglaze enamelled China trade porcelain	1808	3	5,424
13	"Annular wares" pearlware	1805	3	5,415
19	Blue and green edged pearlware	1805	3	5,415
			70	126,430

APPENDIX

Toombs House 1976

Applications of the Mean Ceramic Date Formula (South 1972)

Ceramic type no.	Ceramic type name	Median date	Sherd count	Product

Mean ceramic date = 126,430 ÷ 70 = 1806.1

Sherd count total: 72
Unidentified sherds: 2
Percentage identified: 97

Lightning Source UK Ltd.
Milton Keynes UK
UKHW052139151118
332327UK00013B/220/P